Developing a *Vibrant* Parish Pastoral Council

edited by
Arthur X. Deegan II

PAULIST PRESS
New York / Mahwah, NJ

Library of Congress Cataloging-in-Publication Data

Developing a vibrant parish pastoral council / edited by Arthur X. Deegan II.
    p.   cm.
    ISBN 0-8091-3556-6
    1. Parish councils. 2. Catholic Church—Government. 3. Pastoral
  theology—Catholic Church. I. Deegan, Arthur X.
BX1920.D48 1995
254′.02—dc20   94-39971
                                                CIP

Published by Paulist Press
997 Macarthur Boulevard
Mahwah, New Jersey 07430

Printed and bound in the
United States of America

Contents

Contents

Preface

The Conference for Pastoral Planning and Council Development is the only national Catholic organization that is devoted primarily to the promotion of pastoral planning and the ongoing development of pastoral councils. Its members are for the most part professionals engaged in these ministries or in training others to become involved in them.

Sometimes painfully learned, at other times foreseen through a logical thought process, the connection between planning and consultative bodies has become obvious to those who are involved in this work. It is now accepted that those who plan for any organization must involve that group's members in a participative dialogue if the plan is to be acceptable and successfully implemented. And it is equally recognized that if a collaborative group is to engage in any worthwhile function, planning for its future must be one of its principal activities and expectations.

Nowhere is this more evident than in church work. If the people of God are to live their baptismal call to share in the responsibility of building the church, they must have a role in the planning that will make it happen. And if anyone hopes to have a pastoral plan that will be supported/carried out by the community of faithful, that plan will have to be done in a participative manner.

Unfortunately, some proponents of either a planning system or a collaborative process have forgotten the need to interrelate both of these. For several years the conference has conducted regional workshops in various parts of the country for clergy, religious and laity to underscore the interdependence of pastoral planning and collaborative decision making, under the title "Developing a Vibrant Parish Pastoral Council." Attendees have found the program to be a help in beginning a parish pastoral council from scratch. Others have found in the workshops a way to breathe new life into an existing council.

This volume is a collection of independent chapters treating one or another of the topics found most helpful to these regional workshop participants. Each chapter has been written by a member of the conference specifically for this collection with a view to providing instructional material to a wider audience than those able to attend the conference's regional workshops.

Because the human skills needed for success in parish leadership must be rooted in theological reflection, the first chapter by Father John A. Coleman, Professor of Theology at the Jesuit School of Theology, San Francisco, California, treats of the ecclesiology of pastoral planning. It establishes the principles of Vatican II as the underpinning of both the rationale and the practicum of pastoral planning at the parish level.

The second chapter recounts a brief history of parish councils as they have evolved in the United States (sometimes pastoral and sometimes not). Mr. Dennis O'Leary, Director of the Chancery for the Archdiocese of Seattle, draws upon his years of experience working in a number of different types of parishes to situate the need for parish pastoral councils in both theology and canon law and suggests a transitional model now being practiced as a recommended norm.

"Competing Visions of Pastoral Councils" then presents another view of the plurality of forms which can be legitimately taken by councils. Its author is Dr. Mark F. Fischer, Assistant Professor at St. John's Seminary in Camarillo, California as a result of several years of research of what works and what doesn't at the parish level.

The busy pastor, dealing with a parish staff, long-standing parish organizations and also relatively new canonical structures (such as a Finance Committee), will find concrete advice in the chapter, "A Pastor's View of How a Parish Pastoral Council Should Work," written by Monsignor John F. Murphy, President of the Priests' Council in the Diocese of Covington, Kentucky.

The next two chapters deal with the mechanics often found to be significant stumbling blocks to the successful operation of a parish pastoral council. Dominican Sister Mary Kay Bailey, treats of the selection of council members and illustrates the discernment process as it might be practiced by a parish wishing to call forth leaders. The next chapter then outlines procedures for leaders to employ in reaching out to multiply the number of those involved in parish activities by a process of emPOWERment, with many practical examples given by the Vice Chancellor of the Diocese of Metuchen, Mrs. Eileen Tabert.

Perhaps the most difficult facets of a meaningful parish pastoral council, spirituality and prayer, are dealt with in "Council Spirituality: Foundation of Mission" by Sr. Marie Kevin Tighe, SP, recently retired as Director of the Office for Pastoral Councils for the Archdiocese of Indianapolis. "The Parish Pastoral Council and Prayer" is offered by Sr. Kathleen Turley, RSM, Director of Pastoral Planning and Council Development of the Diocese of Albany, New York. They both address the need to leave room for the Spirit to continually infuse the agenda and deliberations of the parish pastoral council, lest it devolve into one more committee dealing with temporalities, causing frustration on the part of those who expected council work to somehow be a faith enriching experience.

In recognition of the demographics of the church in America today, and the projections for its increasingly multicultural makeup, Nancy M., Pineda, M. Div., Director of Planning for the Archdiocese of Seattle, Washington, describes five models of parish organizations to respond to cultural diversity, and presents several challenges in selecting an appropriate approach to this sore and more complex situation.

"Strategic Pastoral Planning," is a how-to-do-it primer on the skills of planning as applied to pastoral concerns in a parish. In it I have sought to follow the model of strategic planning as practiced in the corporate world.

The last chapter is a reminder that the last step in any formal process is one of evaluation. Marliss Rogers shares the approach she has been using with pastoral councils for many years.

There are other dimensions of what might be called "the care and feeding of parish pastoral councils" that could have been included in this collection. The reader is referred to other volumes which treat of selecting council members, training council members, motivating council members, and so forth. The effort here has been to bring together the fields of organization development and theological reflection with a view to making the experience of those who serve on parish pastoral councils a rewarding one, not only in terms of task accomplishment, but also as answering a call to ministry.

Clearwater, Florida
April, 1994

The Ecclesiology of Pastoral Planning

by John A. Coleman, SJ

One of my Jesuit housemates sports a T-shirt with the bold invective: "Join the Resistance!" Its sub-text reads: "Support Vatican II." The purpose of this chapter is to rehearse the major thrust of Vatican II's understanding of the church and its implications for pastoral planning, parish pastoral councils and consultation in the church. Reviewing Vatican II one more time is important, because as the T-shirt notes, the council is not simply past history but an evocation of a task still to be completed.

Ecclesiology or "thought about the church" was central to the Second Vatican Council. The two most important documents of the council were undoubtedly Lumen Gentium (The Dogmatic Constitution on the Church) and Gaudium et Spes (The Pastoral Constitution on the Church in the Modern World). Sometimes these days people overdo the before and after view of Vatican II. Many of the things Vatican II championed existed in the church and in church movements before the council. Many of the things that existed in the church before Vatican II continue to have validity. But undoubtedly, Vatican II represented a major shift in thinking about the church.

New ideas and metaphors for the church came into being at the council, notably: the Church as a communion, the church as the people of God, the church as the sacrament of the unity of the world, the church as herald. These did not totally displace, of course, older concepts of a visible and institutional church, but relativized them. Yet, as the official commentary on the council's notion of communion made clear, "communion is not to be understood as some vague sort of good will, but as something organic which calls for a juridical structure as well as being enkindled by charity." The church, for all its mystery in grace and God's free call, remains also visible, necessarily so—a juridical structure and institution.

We will first look more deeply into the meaning of that word "communion." We will next discuss collegiality and how it applies to the laity. Then we will take up two other Catholic terms which inspired the council: subsidiarity and justice as participation. After that we will apply these three notions (collegiality, subsidiarity and justice as participation) to planning parish pastoral councils and consultation in the church.

Communion

Angel Anton, a Jesuit who teaches ecclesiology at the Gregorian University in Rome puts his finger on what he thinks was key about the way the church was conceived at Vatican II:

> The concept of communion is without a doubt the key concept for interpreting the ecclesiology of Vatican II and the one that best summarizes its results in ecclesiological doctrine and in the renewal of the Church. The fact of having focused the theology of the mystery of the Church on this concept of koinonia, fellowship, represents perhaps the most transcendent innovation of Vatican II for post-conciliar ecclesiology and the life of the Church. The ecclesiological content of the concept is not absolutely new: rather it is latent in the ideas and models of the Church prior to Vatican II.

Yves Congar had anticipated before the council that, among the positions describing the church, that of communion would hold a central place in the ecclesiology of the future. This prophecy has been fulfilled.

> In fact, beginning with Vatican II, the idea of communion is at the very center of the ecclesiological debate. It

is intimately linked to the other key idea at Vatican II of the people of God which, through the conciliar constitution and decrees, has obtained an important place in Catholic ecclesiology. The ecclesiology of Vatican II began with this key concept of Church—communion of all mankind in Christ and went on to see it actualized in the people of God of the New Covenant, which has Christ as its head in accordance with the universal plan of salvation of the Father, who has revealed himself in a fully open and irrevocable way in the mission of the Son, and, through the mission of the Spirit, preserves its integrity in time and space until the end of time, when God will be all in all.

Communion speaks of unity, a kind of radical bondedness and equality of all believers in a communication of truth and the spiritual goods of the church. Ultimately, the secret of our communion in the church flows from our being joined by Jesus in the communion of life of the Trinity: Father, Son and Spirit, and in our being called to share in Jesus' mission. For whoever says communion also immediately says mission. Our unity as equal baptized, no matter what our rank in the church, flows from being called as disciples to share in the mission of Jesus to proclaim and enable the coming of God's kingdom. The church itself is but a prolongation of the mission and purposes of Jesus. Its unity comes fundamentally from living the life of holiness as disciples. Thus, in a very significant move during the council, the chapter on the equality of all believers in baptism took precedence over the chapter on the hierarchical nature of the church. The second can only make sense inasmuch as it is rooted in and serves the communion of all believers. As Castillo Lara, a Spanish theologian, immediately reminds us:

> At the very heart of the concept of communion is found the concept of participation. Communion is not only a relational bond but also participation in common goods, in the mystery of the Trinitarian communion, in the gifts of the Holy Spirit, in salvation, in charisms in the faith, in hope and charity, in the mission of the Church.

Thus, *Lumen Gentium* insisted that, by virtue of our baptism, all the members of the faithful participate in the threefold ministry of Christ and the church "in accord with the condition proper to each one."

Thus, even though the church is not, formally, a democracy, its theological self-understanding, especially since Vatican II, encourages a deep-going application of a participative ethos to its structures and behaviors. We still suffer, however, a deficit in bringing about the structures which would bring alive the kind of mutual and full participation which lies at the root of Vatican II's thought. The church has its own theory of equality (the equality of the discipleship of equals, the church as common discipleship—one of the models of the church of Avery Dulles), rooted in the notion of a universal priesthood of all believers (you, too, were anointed in baptism with the chrism that a priest is anointed with in ordination). At Vatican II, in the document on the Constitution of the Church, *Lumen Gentium,* the council fathers argue that this fundamental equality of all being equally called to holiness and discipleship takes precedence over hierarchy (which does not mean that it negates hierarchy) as a grounding belief about the church. They preface their treatment of hierarchy by a more encompassing claim about the universal call of all in the church to holiness, rooted in baptism:

> All share a true equality with regard to the dignity and to the activity common to all the faithful (# 32c).

> There is in Christ and in the Church no inequality on the basis of race or nationality, social conditions or sex (# 32b).

Vatican II, then, chose inclusive rather than hierarchical metaphors (communion and people of God) as its primary model for understanding the church.

The sense of freedom which participation gives and presupposes is echoed in Vatican II's declaration on religious freedom (*Dignitatis Humanae*) on the essential freedom of the act of faith. Vatican II also affirms an essential diversity within the church.

> By divine institution, the holy Church is structured and
> governed with a wonderful diversity. . . . This diversity
> among its members arises by reason of their charisms and
> duties (*Lumen Gentium* #13c).

The major impetus for structural reform to broaden consultation and councils in the church derives from the word which
catches the spirit of the definition of the church as a communion in
heart and mind in a common mission and in sharing the common
life of God. That word is collegiality.

Collegiality

The church as collegial communion means that the church is
not an absolute monarchy. It is not a one way street. We are all, and
not just Peter, rightfully in the bark of Peter which, of course, is first
of all the ark of salvation. When Paul VI requested at Vatican II that
the council fathers insert into their schema on the church that the
pope was answerable to God alone, they refused. They did not see
the pope as an absolute monarch. "The pope is the head of the
episcopal college as 'successor' in the apostolic ministry to Peter,
who is head of the college of apostles. As head of the college, he is
relative to other bishops who are members of the same college."
The pope may not abrogate, in this view of the council, the rightful
ordinary authority of bishops in their dioceses who are no less than
the direct successors of the apostles. Bishops remain co-responsible
with the pope for the unity, legitimate diversity and freedom of the
world-church. As Karl Rahner put it succinctly:

> (1) the pope is not an absolute monarch in the political
> sense;
> (2) the episcopate exists always by divine right and not
> by delegation from the pope;
> (3) the papal primacy juridically constitutes the Church
> only when conjoined with the world episcopate; and
> (4) bishops have episcopal power distinct from the pope
> and not delegated by the pope.

The church is not a monarchy but shows a conciliar, ordered collegial structure.

In the Vatican II document on priests, collegiality is extended to apply to the relation of bishops to ordained priests. Priests carry out their ministry in the name of Christ, says the decree Presbyterium Ordinis. Their office is bestowed on them through the sacrament of orders whereby they are able to act "in the person of Christ." Through their ordination, they receive the gift of the Holy Spirit. Thus, the decree on priests instructs bishops to listen to their priests, to ask their advice, to consult with them. Priests are called the bishops' "friends and brothers."

Dutch theologian Peter Huizing captures the independent collegial role of priests in the church and applies it to all who are full ministers in the church. The priest's independent role—and that of deacons and laypeople in pastoral ministry—is determined by their direct link with the local communities in which they work. The bishop's role is clearly different from this. The idea that the pastoral care of parishes and groups of people is entrusted to pastoral workers only because the bishop himself cannot be everywhere at once and do everything himself, though this should be the ideal, is absurd not only as a matter of obvious pastoral experience but also as a matter of principle: the diocesan church, too, only exists in and out of local churches with their own life, and the existence of these demands that they independently have at their own disposal the pastoral ministries they need under the coordination of the bishop.

Collegiality between pope and bishops, between bishops and those who do ministry, also applies to the laity in the church. The Second Vatican Council stresses the rightful autonomy of the laity in the secular order. The hierarchy has neither the ability nor mandate to take upon itself the church's entire mission. We are a collegial communion, all in this bark together, because of baptism; it is everyone's church. The task of the hierarchy, says *Lumen Gentium*, is to provide the ministry of leadership and inspiration for the individual mission of every one of the faithful with his or her abilities or charisms (#30). Lay apostolate is an independent participation in the mission of the church, in which the laity's mission comes from the Lord himself through baptism and confirmation (#33). Laypersons have the right and often the duty to give their judgment on the church's internal affairs (#37).

The revised Code of Canon Law notes that the laity share also in the governing office of Christ. The Christian faithful "have become sharers in Christ's priestly, prophetic and royal office and are called to exercise the mission which God has entrusted to the Church to fulfill in the world, in accord with the condition proper to each one" (Canon 204, #1). Vatican II's decree on the lay apostolate (which called for some form of diocesan and parish councils) points also to the freedom of association of the laity in the church, even for directly apostolic enterprises (*Apostolicam Actuositatem,* #19). Dorothy Day did not need permission to start the Catholic Worker Movement, or Jean Vanier to start L'Arche communities. For at root, as the French theologian Dom O. Rousseau has argued, the idea of the church as a communion, above all signifies koinonia, a free circulation of the same spiritual goods among and between Christian brothers and sisters. Put succinctly, there is no communion without true communication of truths and goods; no communication without collegiality; without participation, without consultation, voice and dialogue. With this strong theology of the church as collegial communion, the only puzzle was not that Vatican II allowed parish and diocesan councils; the only puzzle is that it did not absolutely mandate them!

Subsidiarity

The principle of subsidiarity, first enunciated by Pius XI in his social encyclical *Quadragesimo Anno,* assumes that good order, in any society, depends on preserving the diversity and vitality of local sub-units and genuine communities in that society. As stated by Pius XI, subsidiarity insists that

that which individual men and women can accomplish by their own initiative and their own industry cannot be taken away from them and assigned to the community; in the same way, that which minor or lesser communities can do should not be assigned to a greater or higher community. To do so is a grave injury and disturbance of the social order for social activity by its nature should supply help (*subsidium*) to the members of the social body, never destroy or absorb them.

Subsidiarity favors intermediate associations between the individual and the highest organs of governance in a society. It represents a bias about where real societal creativity is to be found. It assumes that problems are generally best formulated and solved by those who feel them most acutely. Subsidiarity enhances a principle of local freedom and initiative. It enshrines social pluralism in society. Catholic social theory favors, without absolutizing them, decentralized forms of authority.

But does subsidiarity apply to the church? The answer is a decided yes for several reasons. First, what holds true for all and every healthy human community must hold also for that special community called the church. All the more so if we take seriously that the Vatican Council—in the *Church in the Modern World*—used the metaphor of the church as the sacrament for and of the world, which anticipates in its life of communion what the world should have in its communities. Hence, in this view, the church is bound to embody in its own structures what it holds up as the ideal for all good communities. Moreover, the church's authorities themselves have pronounced in favor of an application of subsidiarity to its own structures. In 1946, when addressing the newly appointed members of the college of cardinals, Pius XII noted that the principle of subsidiarity "is valid for social life in all of its organizations and also for the life of the Church." The Vatican commission entrusted with revising the Code of Canon Law was instructed by church authorities to take subsidiarity as a guiding principle for devising law in the church. Karl Rahner justified the episcopal conference as of the essence of the church by an appeal to subsidiarity.

Subsidiarity follows necessarily from truly understanding the universal church as a communion of local churches, a communion of communions. This understanding of the church receives an endorsement at Vatican II:

The Church of Christ is truly present in all legitimate congregations of the faithful which, united to their pastors, are themselves called churches in the New Testament. For in their locality these are the new people called by God, in the Holy Spirit and in much fullness (cf. 1 Thess. 1:8) (*Lumen Gentium* #26).

Social ethicist Johannes Messner sums up the root meaning of subsidiarity. "No social authority, therefore, has a right to interfere with activities for individual and social ends as long as those responsible for those ends are able and willing to cope with them." In the church, no less than society, the role of social authority exists as an instrument to guarantee freedom and the finality of Christian freedom itself.

Messner connects subsidiarity with the common good. "The laws of subsidiarity function and the law of the common good are in substance identical." They are identical because in Catholic thought the common good envisions not only the good of the whole but the good of individuals who comprise the whole as well. In this sense, authority does not replace nor should it interfere with the rights of persons and their legitimate intermediary and local groups. Authority's function is subsidiary: to help the individual and intermediate groups to help themselves, to coordinate groups among themselves. The law of subsidiarity function prescribes that authority act for the common good in accord with the dignity of the human person by allowing men and women and lesser societies through social action to freely pursue their own perfection, diversity and creativity. The freedom and dignity of human persons sets constitutional limits on the powers of authority, even within the church. Subsidiarity, favoring local units and initiative, remains, however, an airy abstraction without genuine structures of dialogue at the local level. Once again, it mandates something like consultation and councils.

Justice as Participation

If subsidiarity links up with the great Catholic notion of the common good, it joins, as well, the newer insistence in Catholic social thought on justice as participation. In this view, it is not enough for individuals to be mere passive recipients of justice. As

Vatican II insists in the document on the *Church in the Modern World,* individuals are also active subjects of history, codeterminants of their societal structures and

> conscious that they are themselves artisans and the authors of the culture of their community. Throughout the world there is a similar growth in the combined sense of independence and responsibility. Such a development is of paramount importance for the spiritual and moral maturity of the human race. (Gaudium et Spes, #55).

Collegiality and subsidiarity, then, link up with a larger sense of justice as participation in any community, even the church. All three underscore participation and the need for consultative and participatory structures. Some might argue that the church is exempt from the norms it proclaims in its social teaching for a just society since it was set up for a supernatural end that transcends the dimensions of this world. This type of argument is not valid. The church, which sees itself as "the sign and sacrament of the unity of the human race" (*Lumen Gentium* #1) claims thereby to be that earthly community that is trying to overcome the visions that impair human unity in the world. Precisely as a sacramental sign, the church must visibly embody that it means to be a just society. Just societies enable and invite the mature participation of all their adult members in the goods of that society, spiritual as well as temporal.

Planning, Parish Councils and Consultation

To this point, we have been talking about the vision of Vatican II and its relation to consultation and councils. We have said little directly about planning. First, Vatican II did not itself say much about planning. But in the post-Vatican II church people have seen that pastoral planning is rooted in a vision of stewardship. Indeed, it is hard to believe that one could improve on Bishop Francis Quinn's rationale for planning in an article in the Sacramento diocesan newspaper, *The Catholic Herald,* where the bishop notes:

Planning is essential in any endeavor. That is particularly true in diocesan ministry. We are living in times when change is accelerating and consequently it is imperative that we foresee the emerging needs of the parishes, the departments of the diocese and of the People of God individually in the years ahead. This will entail making provisions for programs for the diverse ethnic populations of our diocese and to consider the number of clergy and religious we will have in coming years. The Church is a visible institution established by Christ and we must plan, just as He did when He sent His disciples ahead to make provisions for His last paschal meal. Spiritual objectives and goals are the essential work of the Church but in this complex society we must have Church edifices for worship, and educational programs require structures. We must focus on the spiritual essence of the Church but we must take care of our responsibilities to make that ministry a reality in the world. Programs and structures are part of that. Jesus said "If God so clothes the grass in the field which grows today and is thrown into the oven tomorrow, will He not much more provide for you, O you of little faith?" But He also spoke about the need to plan: "What king marching into battle would not first sit down and decide whether with 10,000 troops he can successfully oppose another king advancing on him with 20,000 troops?"

But vision, while important—for without a vision a people perishes—is not enough. What about the structures to embody consultation, collegiality, justice as participation, etc.? Since the Vatican council there have been attempts to embody these values. The synod of bishops was seen as a kind of exercise in collegiality between pope and bishops. The national conferences of bishops also represent collegiality as well as subsidiarity. The American church has built a consultation process into the writing of national bishops' letters. Some dioceses have had pastoral councils and about 40% of the American parishes have parish councils. But it does not seem to have met the demands of the American laity. In a national sample, executed by Gallup, a majority (in each age, gender or socioeconomic category—almost always a two-third's majority) of those over 55 years of age favor the idea that the church should have more democratic decision making at the local, parish, diocesan and Vatican levels.

As we have seen earlier, the council and the new Code of Canon Law recognize that by virtue of their baptisms, all the members of the faithful participate in the threefold ministry of Christ and the church. Although the revised Code of Canon Law makes progress in finding ways to empower the non-ordained to exercise the church's teaching and sanctifying mission (by seeing ministry as something also pertaining to the non-ordained), it does not attend very much or in any very vigorous way to the fact that the participation of the faithful in the governance of the church is no less necessary theologically than their participation in other functions. We can put is this way: "The laity has access but no real voice or participation in decision making."

The Code of Canon Law does recognize the right and at times the duty of all members of the faithful as individuals "to manifest to their sacred pastors their opinion on matters which pertain to the good of the church . . . and to make their opinion known to the other Christian faithful." The church now recognizes freedom of public opinion formation and freedom of assembly in the church. What is lacking, however, are structures and institutions to translate these rights and duties from rhetoric to reality. The pastoral councils whose establishment is recommended in every diocese and permitted at the discretion of the bishop in every parish might help to fill this void. The function of the diocesan pastoral council in the code is "to investigate under the authority of the bishop all those things which pertain to pastoral works, to ponder them and to propose practical conclusions about them" (Canon 511). In the Code of Canon Law, they are seen, then, as policy making bodies. Canon 512 says the members of these councils are clerics, religious and "especially lay persons."

The code sees the diocesan pastoral council as representing the diversity of the diocese. Thus:

> the Christian faithful who are appointed to the pastoral
> council are to be selected in such a way that the entire

portion of the people of God which constitutes the diocese is reflected, with due regard for the diverse regions,
social conditions and professions of the diocese as well as
the role that they have in the apostolate, either as individuals or in conjunction with others.

The code leaves the structuring of parish pastoral councils to local
churches or parishes. However, the nature of the council and the
dynamic of what we called communion suggests that these councils
should also reflect the diversity of the parish community and be or
become truly representative bodies. Nothing prevents a diocese
from stipulating that they be such.

The code leaves to the bishops the question about how members of a diocesan pastoral council are to be designated. They can,
of course, be elected. The *Directory on the Pastoral Ministry of
Bishops* makes a shrewd suggestion:

To make the diocesan pastoral council's work more effective, the bishop can order, if the good of the faithful
requires it, that in every parish, parish pastoral councils
be set up and that these be aligned with the diocesan
pastoral council. These councils, grouped together according to area, could choose their representatives to
serve on the diocesan council, so that the whole diocesan
community may feel that it is offering its cooperation to
its bishop through the diocesan council.

If this suggestion were implemented, this might dispel the parochi-
alism that too often is found in parish pastoral councils. They have
no links outside the parish to the wider diocese. It might also
increase the sense of the constituency they present as members of
the diocesan pastoral council. In canon law, the voice of the diocesan pastoral council is only consultative, but we are reminded by
the *Directory on the Pastoral Ministry of Bishops* "nevertheless the
bishop has great respect for its recommendations, for they offer his
apostolic office the serious and settled cooperation of the ecclesias-
tical community." A similar obligation to consider seriously the
voice of the parish council is, of course, incumbent on pastors.

It is essential that, although diocesan and parish pastoral councils serve as policy directing bodies, that they do not become bogged down simply in Robert's Rules of Order and electoral designs for representativeness. The vision of Vatican II which calls for collegiality, subsidiarity and justice as participation flows from a strongly spiritual vision of our all taking our call to holiness seriously, learning together to read the scriptures and read the signs of the times, seeing our policy making in terms of a mission entrusted to us by Jesus to further his Father's kingdom. Ultimately, such councils call us all to become converted as deep disciples. This is, of course, no easy task as true communion, communication, the building of a community of trust, dialogue and mutual forbearance and support—what Martin Luther King liked to call the beloved community—takes a lifetime.

My suggestion is that people who think about parish pastoral councils also think about their connection with prayer, worship and spirituality. By all means, buy a T-shirt which reads "Join the Resistance—support Vatican II!!" It will take a lifetime of conversion to communion to enact it.

Parish Pastoral Councils: Instruments of Visioning and Planning

by Dennis J. O'Leary

- *What is the role of the parish pastoral council?*
- *What is its relationship to the pastor? to other councils, commissions and organizations of the parish?*
- *What exactly is the work of the council and how is it to go about this work?*
- *What does it mean to be an "instrument of visioning and planning"?*

This chapter is intended to assist pastors and parish pastoral councils, as well as other members of parish staffs and consultative structures, to better understand the purpose, role and responsibilities of the parish pastoral council. It is divided into three parts: 1) a discussion of the historical development of parish pastoral councils, 2) the nature of church governance within which councils operate, and 3) practical suggestions to assist pastors and councils in furthering the mission of the church through pastoral planning. Each section concludes with questions for reflection and dialogue where this is possible.

I. Historical Perspective

Let's first begin with a look at the origins of parish councils. We oftentimes lose sight of the influence our history has on how we operate today. Contemporary parish pastoral councils, once referred to as parish councils, often are captives of historical misunderstandings about their role and function. It might be helpful to review the experience of that history and council development over the last two decades.

The *Decree on the Apostolate of the Laity* from the Second Vatican Council confirmed the responsibility of the laity, through baptism, to actively share in the work of Christ. The laity were particularly challenged to work toward having the spirit of the gospel permeate and improve the temporal order. The decree goes on to say that the laity have an active part of their own in the life and action of the church. The value of sharing responsibility for the mission of the church clearly emerged as a priority.

It was in response to this call that bishops and priests began to look for ways of enabling the laity to better understand and carry out their responsibilities. The parish council emerged as one way to more fully engage parishioners in this work.

Our early councils were often comprised of men whom the pastor trusted, who could give advice, particularly in areas of finance and administration. The meetings were very informal and early parish councils had a very low profile in the parish. My first recollection of a parish council was my father coming home from helping count the collection after mass on Sunday and announcing that Father had asked the group of counters to be his council. During this time, traditional lay parish organizations, the Knights of Columbus, the Altar Sodality, the Holy Name Society, continued to work and seek their direction from the pastor. Parishioners knew they were responsible to help the priests and sisters carry on the ministry of the parish, but had a limited sense of responsibility beyond that.

As councils developed and became more involved in the challenges facing the pastor and the parish, their role began to become more prominent, especially in the areas of finance, organization and even administration. They began to develop their own committee structure. The reason that council agendas focused on these areas seems to relate to both their historical roots (early members were most comfortable in affairs of the temporal order) and the fact that the laity in general still did not see any responsibility for themselves in shaping the pastoral mission of the parish. Were the pastor, for example, to ask the council for a recommendation about the annual parish retreat, none of the members felt any competence or responsibility for discussing something so related to the spiritual health of the parish.

In time, many councils began to play a leadership role as the major coordinating body of the parish, meeting monthly, getting regular reports from parish organizations, sometimes grouping these organizations into commissions, organizing budget processes, scrutinizing annual budgets down to how many pencils will be used in the school this year, etc. In this model, the more historic groups of the parish, the Knights, the Altar Sodality, etc. often resisted such organization, wanting to relate directly to the pastor as they had always done. Some organizations never really fit into the commission structure. There was often a "miscellaneous commission," though not under that name. Council members often questioned the time given to reports, discussions about what seemed like endless details which in the long run did not seem to further the development of the parish or its parishioners.

This model often leads to confusion about the role of the parish council: is it a board of directors? Can it tell commissions and committees what they should be doing? Is it there to arbitrate conflicts among organizations? And what about the pastor? Is the council advisory? Can the pastor veto the council? What about parish staff? Are they responsible to the council? Unfortunately, none of the images conjured up by these questions are helpful in really understanding the role and responsibilities of parish pastoral councils. Many parish councils inappropriately insert themselves into a hierarchical notion of the church and see their ministry in terms of power and authority, while missing the value of shared responsibility and empowerment. Parish pastoral councils are not about power, not about authority, not about supervision, not even about administration.

On this point, consider the following exhortation of the pope as quoted in Origins, Oct. 21, 1993, p. 348:

> The effective participation of the faithful in the church's mission, through parish councils, financial councils, committees for specific activities on both the parish and dioce-

san levels, is an important development in the life of your dioceses," Pope John Paul II said in an address Oct. 2 to a group of U. S. bishops who were making their "ad limina" visits to Rome.

The pope said "It would be an error to judge ecclesial structures of participation and cooperation by secular democratic standards, or to consider them as forms of "power sharing" or means of imposing partisan ideas or interests. They should be looked on as forms of spiritual solidarity proper to the church as a communion.

He said "Such structures are fruitful to the extent that they manifest the true nature of the church as a hierarchical communion animated and guided by the Holy Spirit. When they function according to the Spirit of Christ, they are valid signs of how the baptized bear one another's burdens.

Historical Transition

In order to truly understand the role of the parish pastoral council, we need to be willing to suspend some of our notions about what a council is about, and sometimes even suspend our current agenda and meeting pattern in order to examine other ways of being a council.

The pre-Vatican II model for understanding our church was hierarchical: the pope, the bishops, the priests, religious and laity, all neatly organized on a pyramid, like the organization chart of a corporation. Since the council, many now picture the church as a circle of believers who share responsibility for the mission of the church. The reality is that neither image alone fully reflects the truth of our church. We are a church that is ordered, that clearly distinguishes between the role of the ordained and the role of the laity, but at the same time states that the responsibility for the mission of the church is shared by the entire body. A church faithful to our tradition is not the bishop or clergy in isolation from the faithful, nor the faithful in isolation from the bishop and clergy. The responsibility for the mission of the church is shared by the entire body. New models of pastoral councils are emerging from parishes and dioceses across the country which give new vision and new meaning to their role, and which reflect an ordered church that stresses the responsibility of all for its mission.

Because we are searching for new models to reflect this reality of church, we have been and continue to be in a time of transition. All transitions are marked with a number of feelings and behaviors. We usually have feelings of uncertainty, knowing that our past experience is changing and yet not knowing exactly what the future will look like. We want to hold onto the way we've done things but also know intuitively that they no longer are working. These transitional times are often times of exploring new ways of doing things. On the one hand this requires a great deal of flexibility, but on the other hand we need to ensure that these new efforts are consistent with our tradition. This time is challenging, but within this challenge is truly a gift: these times offer tremendous opportunities for growth, both individually and collectively.

Another Perspective on Parish Pastoral Councils

What if parish councils could be instruments for enabling parishes to serve the needs of their parishioners, the local geographic community, the national and world community? What if the parish pastoral council could give voice to the needs, the hopes, the dreams of its members and empower the parish to create new initiatives? What if the council could be the vehicle for establishing parish priorities that build on the gospel, our tradition, our national bishops' conference and local priorities?

The next section will address some theological and canonical contexts which will help us better understand the function of parish pastoral councils. The last section will outline a new model and new understandings of the role of parish pastoral councils and how that role might be played out.

But first, take time to reflect on and discuss the following questions as they apply to your parish pastoral council:

1. *What is your perception of the current role of your parish pastoral council? What has the council done that contributes to your perception?*

2. *Are roles and responsibilities among the pastor, the parish pastoral council and the other organizations of the parish clear? Are they commonly known and understood among the people of the parish?*
3. *How significant a role do you think the parish pastoral council has played in the ongoing development of parish life? In what areas of parish life?*
4. *How satisfied are you with your current experience of the council? What is most satisfying? What is least satisfying?*

II. Church Governance

The previous section focused on the historical development of parish pastoral councils and some of the transition phenomena we are experiencing. Many councils, despite the inherent frustrations, continue to operate as administrative boards or organizational coordinators of parish life. But many bishops, pastors and lay leaders are working toward a new understanding of the role of parish pastoral councils—councils that could be instruments of visioning and pastoral planning. In this new understanding the council becomes a means for articulating the dreams and needs of parishioners and the community they serve and developing a pastoral plan which responds to these dreams and needs. But this vision is only achievable if council members are willing to build upon and move beyond their current ways of operation.

The documents of the Second Vatican Council and the recently promulgated revised Code of Canon Law have challenged us to a new way of thinking in regard to church structures and governance. However, many of us bring attitudes about participation and decision making from our secular society to our participation in church that are at odds with our theological and canonical foundations. We bring assumptions and attitudes formed from our experience in the business, political or civic world, when in fact we need to bring new assumptions and new attitudes.

In this section we will explore the different perspectives we bring to church governance, review a theological and canonical perspective of church governance and how it differs from the day-to-day models of participation and decision making with which we live, and provide an introduction to a new vision of the role of the parish pastoral council.

The Perspective We Bring

It is difficult to appreciate a new way of thinking about church governance unless we fully appreciate the ways we usually think about organizations and decision making. Most of us, knowingly or unknowingly, approach life with a set of attitudes and assumptions about organizations. Because they are so ingrained in our thinking, we may unwittingly transpose those attitudes and assumptions to our work on councils or other consultative structures in which we participate. Some examples might prove helpful.

We may be used to operating from a **political** perspective or model: building coalitions, working toward a majority, being comfortable with win-lose situations. If one loses, we simply work to gain the majority the next time around. While this model has served our political structures well, it is not a model which supports the development of consensus toward pastoral priorities, involvement of broad constituencies, or promotes unity amidst diversity that more characterizes our church.

Or we may be used to operating from a **business** perspective: compromise and negotiation, with your own interests or that of your business as a fundamental concern. In discussions with unions or potential partnerships, it's a matter of of trading this for that, rather than building a common platform or agreement. Such a model, while perhaps appropriate within the business community, does not support the values or mission of the church.

Again, we may be used to operating from a **civic** model: the most involved are those who have the most power and influence. The uninvolved are seen as problematic and a person's influence is directly related to his/her involvement. In a church context, the model does not allow for the reality that members of our church are at different places in their journey and that this must be respected. The gospel parable that speaks of those hired in the last hour being paid the same as those hired earlier in the day is an example of how Jesus challenges our mindsets.

The models noted above are commonplace to us. These models serve their purposes well: the political model has enabled expedient and peaceful transitions of power, the business model has served to stimulate a world economy, the civic model has spawned neighborhood and community development. But they are not adequate expressions of church governance.

Church Governance

Church governance is quite different from these models. Let's explore some of the theological and canonical foundations which underlie the work of parish pastoral councils, which shape a new way of thinking about councils, as well as introduce how pastoral planning and research can provide focus for parish pastoral councils.

Theological and Canonical Foundation

All of our efforts should be patterned after the mission and ministry of Jesus Christ and the gospel. The early mission of Jesus was to proclaim the Good News of God's saving love for all people, to establish a prayerful community of believers, and to give practical expression to the gospel by serving the needs of others. At baptism each member of the church assumes responsibility to carry forward this mission of Christ in partnership with other church members. Some of the baptized are called to serve the community as ordained ministers who have special responsibility to preach the gospel, to celebrate the eucharist and other sacraments, and to lead the Christian faithful.

A theological context for parish pastoral councils must begin with an understanding of the unique character of the parish. For most Catholics, family and parish provide the most immediate experience of the parish. The parish provides for the partnership we are called to assume with other church members for carrying forward the mission of the church. No parish is an island. No community can pursue the mission in isolation from the universal church. Parishes which make up a diocese are linked with other parishes under the diocesan bishop. Dioceses, through their bishops in communion with the Holy Father, form the Roman Catholic

Church as a whole. Parishes, then, are called to be vehicles for Christian transformation, enabling people to live their lives in the world as the mission given them by Christ. Because it is a community of the faithful, it is essential that the parish structures, including the parish pastoral council, serve the community in carrying out the mission of the church.

Within this theological framework, the Code of Canon Law defines some of the roles that various ministers execute in church governance. Canon 519 states:

> The pastor . . . exercises pastoral care over the community entrusted to him under the authority of the diocesan bishop, in whose Ministry of Christ he has been called to share. In accord with the norm of law, he therefore carries out for his community the duties of teaching, sanctifying and governing with the cooperation of other priests or deacons and the assistance of lay members of the Christian faithful.

Second Vatican Council documents including *Lumen Gentium,* the *Dogmatic Constitution on the Church,* and the *Decree on the Apostolate of the Laity,* emphasize that the laity are called upon to assist the pastor in the pastoral care of God's people and in the administration of the temporal goods of the church.

Two principles that receive emphasis in the code are, 1) the authority entrusted to the hierarchy, and 2) the call for shared responsibility. These two values may seem at odds with one another unless they are understood in light of two other values embraced by church governance: servant leadership and consultation.

Servant Leadership
In the worlds of politics, business and civic society, leadership and authority are often expressed as the ability to assert one's power and influence. Pastoral leadership, in contrast, is a ministry of service. While bishops and priests are to ensure faithfulness to church law and tradition, they are also called to be servants, enabling all parishioners to participate more fully in the life and mission of the parish. Clearly, the responsibility for the mission of

the church is shared by the entire body with bishops and priests called to nurture the community's ability to be that sacred sign of God's presence in the world. And servant leadership is also a challenge to parishioners who serve in parish leadership roles. They must exercise the kind of leadership that enables and empowers others rather than wielding their own power and influence.

Consultation

Consultative structures, such as parish pastoral councils, are a significant means for the church to give practical expression to shared responsibility. Consultative bodies establish a structure whereby the church—clergy and laity—attempt to listen to the Spirit who is leading the church and speaking to her through the gifts and experience of all parishioners, as well as through office and ordination. The term consultative is not meant to diminish its importance. On the contrary, it inserts the body in the governance of the parish at a critical level and charges it with an important responsibility in pastoral planning.

The principles of servant leadership and consultation speak to the need for a different attitude or perspective when exercising authority and participating in parish leadership. They challenge all the people of God to a new understanding of and belief in a theology of grace; that God is present and active in human life, that God is with the church as guide, helper and the ultimate power behind all its efforts. These principles challenge all pastoral leadership to a spirit of selflessness. They call all of us to be responsible for the mission of the church.

Parish Pastoral Planning

In light of the lessons from our history, in light of the theological and canonical realities discussed in this section, a new vision of parish pastoral council is emerging. Not a council that presumes to be a board of directors; not a group that spends most of its time and energies on parish finances (in fact, the new Code of Canon Law assigns many of these consultative responsibilities to the parish Finance Council); not a council that provides management or administrative functions. Instead, a council which is a vehicle for the parish to develop a clearer and deeper understanding of the need for all to share in the responsibility to carry on Christ's mission in the world; a council which listens to the people of the parish, assesses the needs in their local, regional and world community, studies church teaching, (including the pastoral letters of our bishops and the Pope), and recommends goals and priorities in the shape of a long-range pastoral plan.

The next section will address parish pastoral planning and the leadership roles of the pastor and parish council in this effort. But before that, it may be helpful to stop and reflect on some of the themes raised in this section. Some questions for reflection are:

1. *What is your experience of the assumptions and attitudes which members of your parish pastoral council bring to deliberations?*
2. *What orientation has taken place to deepen your parish pastoral council's awareness of the theological and canonical contexts within which they are called to function?*
3. *How have the values of servant leadership and consultation taken root in the deliberations of your parish pastoral council?*
4. *What are the forces that are moving the council to a new way of thinking about its role in service to the parish? What is holding you back?*

III. The Work of Parish Pastoral Councils

In the first section we reviewed the historical development of parish pastoral councils. We traced the role of the council from an informal advisor to the pastor, to a more public role closely associated with financial and administrative coordination of parish activities. We noted the pitfalls of this, the most common view of council work, and how the experience of pastors and council members called for a new understanding of the role of parish pastoral councils.

In the second section, we reviewed the theological and canonical contexts within which councils operate. We examined the influence of political, business and civic attitudes and assumptions transposed onto church governance and how these perspectives can be inappropriate given the work of the parish pastoral council. We stressed the importance of the principles of servant leadership and consultation.

In this section we will examine more closely the authentic role of the parish pastoral council and specifically how the council might more fully realize its potential in developing and empowering parish life through pastoral planning. We will examine the decision making processes of the council as well as the need for parish pastoral councils to be relevant to the needs of their parishes.

Pastoral Planning

Since the Second Vatican Council, laity, religious, deacons, priests and bishops have come to a clearer and deeper understanding of the need for all to share in the responsibility to carry on Christ's mission in the world. Pastoral planning draws on the insights, commitment, vision and awareness that come from the Spirit of God speaking through the Christian faithful, while insuring fidelity to revelation and the teachings that come to us from the magisterium of the church. Parish pastoral councils can play a significant leadership role in pastoral planning efforts.

Pastoral planning is a term which umbrellas four different functions:

The first is **organization development:** how do we as a parish determine our mission, our goals and our priorities, within the parameters set forth in church tradition and canon law, and be responsive to the unique needs, hopes and dreams of our parish community? This includes determining who we are, what we're about, what directions we ought to take, how to best allocate resources and develop programs to meet present and future challenges.

The second is **systems design:** what is the relationship of pastor, staff, pastoral council, finance council, commissions, etc; in terms of a planning process? What are their roles and how do they interrelate, plan and operate as a "system" rather than as discrete bodies? How does the parish relate to the diocese and the community at large?

The third area is **research:** how can we use the disciplines of research, demographic and attitudinal research, and program evaluation, to ground our planning in accurate analysis of what is being accomplished today?

The final area is **theological reflection:** in a spirit of prayer and discernment, what is it that all the above information is saying to us about our mission and ministry? What is God trying to say to us through all this? How are these other secular disciplines lived out in light of the gospel and church teaching? This is what makes the parish planning be pastoral: we analyze and make decisions for the good of souls.

The Pastoral Planning Process

There are a number of levels at which parishes do planning. Most parishes have experience in planning programs and events. Many parishes do planning on an administrative level, assigning ministerial resources, preparing budgets, etc. While this type of planning is important, the focus for parish pastoral councils is not in these areas, but in directional and strategic pastoral planning.

Directional planning results in statement of mission and direction. Who are we? What is our unique identity within the context of the diocesan and universal church? What are our priorities? Directional planning requires being familiar with and faithful to church teaching and the mission of the larger church, and a willingness and ability to listen to the people of the parish. This listening process, in the spirit of servant leadership, should give voice to the hopes, the needs, the dreams of parishioners.

Strategic planning and strategic decisions focus more on specific issues or areas of concern. Strategic decisions are those which result in the commitment of major ministerial and financial resources. Strategic decisions generally take months and years to achieve their intended results, and once made are difficult to reverse.

It is the primary responsibility of the parish pastoral council to assist the pastor in directional and strategic planning. If planning in these two areas is done well, administrative and program planning by the pastor, staff, and program leaders will naturally follow and the result will be a more focused and integrated approach to ministry. The pastoral planning process might be viewed as a sequence of lenses which further refine and focus the work of the parish.

In order for pastoral planning to be done well, consultation with the parish membership, leadership and staff by the pastoral council are essential to the integrity of the process. As the pastor consults with the council, so the council itself is called to consult with parish leadership and parishioners in general.

So what might a parish pastoral planning process look like? The pastor and the council would begin by determining what universal, national, and local church documents would be appropriate to study to inform the planning process. They will determine a method of listening to the people of the parish: parish meetings, district meetings in homes, telephone interviews, surveys, home visitations or combinations of the above. They may identify other sources of information that could inform the process, information about the needs of the geographic area and what services are already provided. Through prayer, study and listening a mission statement is developed. Through their deliberations, possible goals and priorities will begin to emerge. These alternatives need to be tested with parish staff and leadership to determine which of these priorities need to be tested with parish staff and leadership to determine which of these priorities seem to the most timely, which ones garner the most commitment. Once the council finalizes its recommendations to the pastor and the pastor authorizes a set of goals and priorities, they should be published and celebrated.

The council then begins to work with parish staff and leadership to develop possible strategies for achieving the goals. If a statement regarding evangelization is a priority, strategies that might be examined include conducting a parish census, adopting a returning catholics program, assigning additional resources to the preparation of adults for entry into the church. For every priority there will be host of possible strategies. Once a consensus is achieved about strategies, the pastor, working with staff and program leaders, completes the pastoral planning process through administrative and program planning. While many councils involve themselves in administrative planning and administration, the result is inevitably frustration on everyone's part. No group, meeting monthly, can be effective at managing day-to-day administration. If you, as a council, are finding yourselves concerned about such issues as how to stripe the parking lot, it's a good indicator you're working in the wrong area. You should be much more concerned about who are parking their cars, what their needs, hopes and dreams are. At the end of the planning process, the pastor and council will need to develop some systems for evaluating whether the priorities are being achieved.

Consensus

Effective pastoral planning is dependent upon an effective decision making process which is inclusive and works toward building a common foundation for commitment to a direction. Consensus building is critical to this process. It often times requires a new attitude, a selflessness, a posture of searching for the common point of agreement. Attitudes discussed in the last section—the political (win-lose) posture, the business model of negotiation and compromise, the civic model which credits membership and involvement—will not work well in consensus building. Within the context of faithfulness to the teachings of the church, parish pastoral planning should use consensus processes which will promote community and a commitment to the gospel and our faith tradition.

Consensus does not imply unanimity (that is, everyone's first choice). But it does indicate substantial commitment to a direction. In working toward consensus, various process tools are available to assist groups in determining which alternatives have the greatest underlying support. In the end, it is the council that must determine if there is enough commitment to finalize its recommendations to the pastor. The process can be time consuming but the commitment generated makes that time invaluable, and saves time in trying to get ownership or buy-in after the decision has been made.

A Reality Check

As we move toward ending this section, it is important to mention doing a "reality check." Parish pastoral councils must be about real-life issues if they are to be of assistance to the pastor in furthering the mission of the church in their parish. The people of your parish have real hopes, dreams, needs. Councils need to develop goals and priorities that address these real needs.

For example, we need to find ways to strengthen our faith communities in light of the changes around us. Our liturgies need to be vibrant. Many Catholics are searching to deepen their prayer life and spirituality. Many of our parishes are becoming more complex, more diverse racially, culturally, economically. There are challenges that require the emergence of greater local leadership. Vocations to the priesthood and lay ministries come from the parish.

National and local research continues to indicate that passing on our tradition is a major concern to Catholics. Parishioners want to better understand their faith, and they want their children to understand and appropriate the faith. Our church continues to be an immigrant church. We need to find ways to assist these immigrants in maintaining their faith traditions, support their family life, and assist them in their transition. We need to focus on priorities that address this complex issue.

A final area addresses justice and service. This is an area that requires education and study as well as action. Will your parish's priorities include the homeless, hurting families, the hungry, those with disabilities, those with addictions, the disenfranchised, the aging, those facing unwanted pregnancies? The list goes on. . . .

Conclusion

The challenges to the pastor and parish pastoral council may seem overwhelming: to grasp our history and understand its impact on our operations, to understand the theology of councils and how the Code of Canon Law provides parameters and insights into council operations, to examine the appropriate and significant role of the council and to ensure it works effectively and addresses real-life issues. These challenges may seem overwhelming. But the good news is the Good News: we are not alone. Through God's grace, our work, as imperfect as it might be, can lead to furthering the mission of the church and the kingdom of God. We don't have to do it all. Your parish doesn't have to touch every area. There are parishes around you that share common needs, hopes and dreams.

You are part of a diocese that can provide for communication and planning at a broader level, and can address goals and priorities that an individual parish would not have the resources to address.

A reading from the first letter of Peter sums up our call and puts forth a message of hope in such clear terms in our time:

> We possess the prophetic message as something altogether reliable. Keep your attention closely fixed on it as you would on a lamp shining in a dark place until the first streaks of dawn appear and the morning star rises in your hearts.

That your parish pastoral council might be a source of light and grace for your parish, you might wish to reflect upon the following questions about topics covered in this last section:

1. *In which aspects of pastoral planning (organization development, system design, research and theological reflection) does your parish pastoral council have some experience? How satisfying has that experience been?*
2. *In what areas of parish life and planning has your parish pastoral council been most involved: directional, strategic, administrative and/or programmatic? What has been your experience of the council's agenda?*
3. *How does your council come to decisions? What attitudes seem to be present during deliberations?*
4. *What significant issues do you feel the council has addressed? What issues, appropriate to the council's delegation, are faced by your parish that have not been part of the council's agenda?*

Competing Visions
of Pastoral Councils

by Mark F. Fischer, Ed.D.

If I were a pastor who wished to establish or renew a parish council, I would be confused by a survey of current literature. There are several books about pastoral councils currently in print, but little consensus about councils themselves. Unless a pastor had considerable experience with councils, he would not know how to discriminate among the competing recommendations by the published experts.

I am not a pastor, but I have had experience with councils as a diocesan administrator who assisted them for six years. Now, as a seminary professor, I teach about them. To be sure, I will never see councils from a "pastor's-eye view." But unlike many pastors, I have the leisure to read what is published about councils and offer my interpretation. Here I voluntarily take the standpoint of a pastor, because pastors are in a position to establish or renew councils. The laity usually are not.

In this chapter, I will first give some examples of the diverse recommendations for councils which have been recently published. Next, I will offer a critique based on experience, suggesting why some recommendations are unrealistic and unworkable. Then I will present a synthesis of the literature and a definition of the council ministry. In my opinion, the published literature confronts councils with competing visions. The final section states why I believe the visions are not of equal value.

Diverse Recommendations

Let us begin with some of the diverse recommendations for pastoral councils. Diversity in itself is not a bad thing. But when diverse recommendations contradict one another, a problem arises. And in the areas of committee structure, initiative, and member selection, significant contradictions about pastoral councils do exist.

Committee Structure

The first and, to my mind, the greatest problem, has to do with the council's committee structure. Some publications recommend that parish councils have a full-blown structure of standing committees. The purpose of such a structure is to plan and coordinate the overall policy of the parish.[1] The pastoral council's main job is to coordinate parish ministry through the committees. For that reason, the council is called a "council of ministries."[2] Through its ministry committees, the council makes a concrete impact on the parish.

But other publications recommend that pastoral councils should *not* have an extensive committee structure. They regard the maintenance of ministries as an administrative task for the parish staff. The main task of the council, from this viewpoint, is pastoral reflection and planning.[3] Although communicating about the variety of ministries is important, it is not primary. Discernment of mission comes first.[4] Councils that spend most of their time coordinating committees usually have little time for pastoral planning and discernment.

Pastoral Initiative

If the committee structure is the foremost problem area, the second area has to do with pastoral initiative. Some publications suggest that the council (with the pastor as one among other members) should take the initiative in pastoral council agendas. If the wisdom of the parish community resides in the council, they say, the council should be the decision maker. The role of the pastor is a limited one: to participate with the council in its search for truth.[5] The council makes the decisions; he ratifies them by his presence and participation.[6] In the interest of promoting lay leadership, initiative belongs to the council.

Other publications, however, express the pastor's role in stronger terms. He is the parish authority, the one at the center of the neighborhood church, the depositor of the people's vision. He realizes this authority in service to the community. The council is the group he consults to evaluate and recommend improvements, but not to implement the recommendations.[7] They advise but do not administer. He involves them in pastoral planning, sharing responsibility with them.[8] Pastoral council initiative is first his before it is theirs.

Selection of Councilors

A third major area of contention concerns the selection of councilors. Most guidelines for parish councils published by dioceses recommend that councilor selection be "representative."[9] By this they usually mean what canon 512 in the 1983 code says about diocesan pastoral councils, namely, that members be selected in such a way "that the entire portion of the people of God which constitutes the diocese is truly reflected." True, all councilors should put the good of the parish first, say the guidelines. But they do this by representing different constituencies. For this reason they should reflect the demographic profile of the parish.

In contrast to those who stress "representation" are those who stress the "discernment" of gifts. When discerning council membership, what counts is not having the right demographic profile but rather attracting those who are particularly gifted for council work—regardless of their race, gender, or culture.[10] From this viewpoint, nomination by others and election by the parish as a whole are unnecessary. Far more important are a discernment of God's call and a testing of that call by those who share a concern for it.

Competing Visions

Each of the alternatives we have presented springs from a different vision of the council. The council of ministries sees itself as an instrument of lay involvement. It ensures a variety of ministries in the parish, staffed by lay volunteers, all supported by the council. The pastoral planning council, by contrast, presents another vision. It is the vision of a parish focused on its mission. Such a council is less interested in the maintenance of present ministries than in the assessment of needs and in planning a response to them. For one council, the focus is lay involvement in the present. For the other, the focus is the future.

The alternatives of "pastor" and "council" initiative also present competing visions. An emphasis on council initiative springs from a vision of lay leadership. Vatican II called for shared responsibility in the church, and allowing councils to make decisions very definitely gives them responsibility. A quite different vision underlies the emphasis on pastor initiative. It is the vision of the pastor as spiritual leader, the one whose direction calls forth and orders the gifts of the community. In this vision, the pastor asks the council to reflect on a given issue and facilitates the search for consensus. In the other vision, the council is the sphere of lay leadership.

Our final set of alternatives—representation versus discernment—suggests still other visions. When we emphasize the council as a representative of the parish community, we envision it offering the pastor the wisdom of the parish in microcosm. In a representative council, no element of the parish is ignored. Every constituency is present. But when we emphasize the discernment of members for the council, another vision is present. It is the vision of the council as a group of gifted people, chosen for a particular ministry by those who know what the ministry entails. In the representative council, the vision is democratic. In the council whose members are chosen by discernment, the vision is charismatic.

A Critique of Council Literature

Our hypothetical pastor may well scratch his head in puzzlement as he reviews the contradictory visions outlined above. The question of which alternative to choose is difficult. Each vision champions values which are worth preserving.

Indeed, our pastor may well object at this point: those so-called alternatives or contradictory positions are not necessarily in contradiction. One can have both standing committees and pastoral planning, council initiative and pastor initiative, representation and discernment. It seems unnecessarily provocative to call them contradictions.

To this objection I would say this: the paired recommendations above are not logically but practically in contradiction. Given the limited time available to a volunteer council, given the limited human resources available to the parish, choices have to be made. In my experience, the diverse recommendations in the published literature do in fact become alternatives. Either a parish council will spend its time coordinating ministries or planning for the future. Either the council will view itself as a policy-making administrative group or a reflective body of consultors. Councilor selection will emphasize either representativeness or the discernment of gifts. One can have both in theory—but in practice, one or the other alternative usually takes first place.

A choice between the alternatives cannot be argued strictly on the basis of abstract principles. There are no criteria which are always and everywhere true by which to choose. Any choice has to be made on the basis of experience. And in what follows, I would like to offer choices based on my experience.

The Council of Ministries?

If I were a pastor, I would avoid the "council of ministries" approach.[11] According to this approach, the pastoral council coordinates the work of standing committees or commissions, setting policy and delegating to each commission the issues which fall within its purview. To me, this is a mistake on three counts.[12] First, ministry will continue whether the parish council is coordinating it or not. Second, the coordination of all parish ministry is beyond the scope of a volunteer group which meets two hours per month. Third, policy setting and delegation are administrative tasks which do not harmonize with the consultative role of the pastoral council. The "council of ministries" approach too closely resembles the management style of a city council.

In its place, I would recommend the pastoral planning approach.[13] This approach focuses the council on pastoral planning and leaves implementing to the staff and to parish committees independent of the council. It is more modest in scope and realistic in expectation than the council of ministries. It makes the consultative nature of the pastoral council clear. And it may improve the parish by separating evaluation from implementation. After all, a council hardly can be neutral when it evaluates the programs which it has implemented itself.

Ratifying by Participation?

A pastor who wants to establish or renovate a parish council must be a strong leader. For that reason, I take issue with those who view the pastor as the "ratifier" of council decisions.[14] According to this viewpoint, the pastor's role is to endorse in the name of the diocesan church what the council, as the voice of the parochial people of God, has decided. This minimizes the pastor's role as "presider" in the council, I would say, and downplays the consultative nature of the council's work.[15]

A genuine pastor is more than a participant in the council. He communicates his vision to the group not merely by his excitement and enthusiasm, as some suggest, but by leadership. He ought to be the one who actively consults the council by defining problems, exploring solutions, and deliberating which solution is best for the community.[16] This is not clericalism or authoritarianism. It is leadership. A good pastor focuses a task, frees the gifts of councilors, and in this way shapes the mission of the parish.

A Representative Council?

Finally, if I were a pastor, I would downplay the idea of a "representative" council. Although the council is widely heralded in diocesan guidelines as a representative body, nevertheless an overemphasis on its representational aspect can lead to an abuse of council members' gifts. We abuse people when we elect them to the council without providing them or us with opportunities to test whether they have a real gift for the council ministry. Instead of using the gifts of councilors to develop pastoral plans and solve pastoral problems, we subject them to what Bertram Griffin calls "the growing sense of boredom on parish super councils where the only action month after month is hearing reports from committees, commissions, and organizations, each having a reserved seat on the board."[17] Qualification for a ministry is more important than ensuring that the council has so many members of this parish organization, race, or culture.[18]

Instead of worrying about demographic profiles, pastors who want a council for needs assessment and planning should create opportunities for reflective people to come forward. That means first clarifying the role of the council, inviting people to see what the council ministry entails, and then asking interested people to help discern who is really called by God to the ministry.[19] In short, we must start with an understanding of council work as a ministry for those with particular gifts. Councilors must have an ability to study a problem, formulate responses to it, and then judge which responses are best. These gifts can best be reckoned by those who understand them and the council. For that reason, the practice of parish-wide election of councilors to ensure "representation" is much less important than we think.

Defining the Ministry

In this chapter, I first sketched some of the contradictions or alternatives presented in current literature on pastoral councils. Then I offered a critique of the alternatives. I argued that they are not of equal value. Indeed, some of them lead to serious mistakes. But the mistakes we have made in promoting councils have a positive effect: they teach us what the council ministry is *not.* Now I would like to say what the ministry *is.* I can summarize my definition under three headings: purpose, scope, and gifts.

First, the ministry of the council is pastoral planning. That is its main purpose.

Second, the ministry extends to practical matters, to what is true for a particular people in a particular parish. That is its scope.

Third, the ministry of the council is charismatic. By that I mean that councilors require special gifts and that the ministry of the council is itself a gift.

In this final section, I propose that we view our ministry as pastoral planning which discerns practical wisdom through the gift of dialogue.

Pastoral Planning

Let us begin with pastoral planning. Pastoral planning is the main reason for having a pastoral council.[20] The council does pastoral planning when it shares with the pastor its experience of the parish, when it identifies needs, when it studies problems and the various solutions to them, and finally when it recommends to the pastor a particular solution or course of action.[21] It helps the parish see where it is and where it should be going. This is what we mean by the mission of the parish. When the council does pastoral planning, it provides the parish with a clear mission.

This pastoral planning role for the parish council is sanctioned by official church documents—something which cannot be said about those proposals which would have the council be the chief policy-maker of the parish or the administrative coordinator of all parish ministries. The pastoral planning role is also realistic for a volunteer group which only meets for a few hours monthly. But the main argument for the pastoral planning model is *not* that it is officially sanctioned and realistic. Rather, it is that the pastoral planning model allows the parish council to contribute to the governance of the parish. And it does so in the context of participative management.

Participative Management is familiar from the world of business. In a well-managed organization, members participate in that management. By participating, they understand better what the organization is trying to do and are motivated to attain its objectives.[22]

Translating the idea of participative management into the language of church, we can say that the pastoral council clarifies the Christian mission and builds commitment to it. This is the first leg

of participative management. The other leg is parishioner motivation. When pastors utilize the parish council as a pastoral planning
body, they not only get good advice, but they get increased commitment. Councilors are more committed to a mission they define
together because it is their own and because they have had a say in
how the parish shall achieve it.[23] Mission and motivation are the
strong legs upon which the council as pastoral planner stands.

Practical Wisdom

When we speak of pastoral planning as the main reason for
having a council, we are talking about the council's purpose. Now
let us turn our attention from purpose to scope, the second part of
our definition of council ministry. By scope I mean the realm of
council operation, its area of competence. The scope of the pastoral council is practical wisdom.

Practical wisdom is a term from Aristotle's Nicomachean Ethics.[24] It refers not to those truths which are always and everywhere
true, such as the truths of natural science and mathematics, but to
the wisdom in practical matters which depends on a community.
There is no "always and everywhere" answer to questions about
today's most urgent need, about what will work best for this community, and about what God is asking of us in our present situation. The way to get at these questions is not by consulting an
expert, for experts do not know the parish as well as those who live
in it. Instead, we get at the questions of practical wisdom by discussing them with one another.

This is the particular competence of the parish council. Pastors do not turn to councils when they want expert opinions in
moral theology, architecture, or educational methods. They turn
to councils to learn the needs of people and what strategies will
best meet those needs. And about this councilors have something
to say. Their practical wisdom helps the pastor see what is most
urgent and what will work.

The pastor has the decisive role, I believe, in the success of the
parish council. Why? Because he poses the questions. He is the
one who can most effectively direct the council's attention. He has
the main responsibility for the parish. Perhaps one might think

that, in the name of developing lay leadership, a pastor should take a relatively passive stance, allowing the council to develop its own agenda. Perhaps one might think that, for the sake of empowering the laity, he should disempower himself. I disagree.

Councils exist to help pastors confront pastoral problems, weigh solutions to them, and make wise decisions. If pastors let the council develop its own agenda, they may find it going where the council is most at ease, and not where the parish needs help.[25] To pastors I say: lead the council in prayer, build a climate of trust, and share with the council your concerns about the parish. Unburden your hearts about the main problems of the parish. In this way, you can open those problems up and see what kinds of solutions might work.

Ultimately, the role of the pastor in the council is to assume the mantle of Socrates, the Greek philosopher who had a special kind of wisdom. Unlike his adversaries, who believed they had all the answers, Socrates at least recognized the limits of his knowledge. He knew that he did not know all. And this Socratic knowledge is not weakness, but strength. By recognizing the limits of his knowledge, Socrates knew what questions to ask. By asking questions, he empowered his friends to get at the truth.[26]

When the pastor accepts the mantle of Socrates, he empowers the council. He unveils the areas in which more reflection is needed. Doubtless by asking questions he is, like Socrates, confessing the limits of his knowledge. But he is also opening the door to mission, letting light and fresh air into a room that may have been too long closed up, and inviting the council to turn its mind to the parish's most urgent problems. He is inviting it to exercise practical wisdom.

The Charism of the Council

Practical wisdom defines the scope of the council, just as pastoral planning defined its purpose. This brings me to the third and last part of my definition of council ministry. I have argued that councils are more successful as pastoral planners than as coordinators of a system of ministries, and that practical matters are the realm of the council's competence, not technical or administrative matters. All of this presupposes that the council has a particular gift, the ability to reach the truth in conversation. This is what I call the charismatic aspect of council ministry. It means that being on the council requires particular charisms or gifts. Further, one can identify and call forth those gifts in particular ways. And when the parish does so, the council itself becomes a gift, a gift which is ordered to the good of the community.

Let us begin with the gifts which a councilor needs. If we take seriously what I have said about the council as a pastoral planning body, a body whose main task is to discern the practical good for the parish community, then this will have consequences for councilor selection. Planning takes patience, a willingness to reflect, and a desire to listen. The impatient parishioner, the one who wants to rush a judgment and "get on with the job," the parishioner whose mind is made up in advance—this parishioner lacks the gifts necessary for a council member.[27]

But how do we know who has the gift, and how do we get them to join the council? The best opportunity to welcome the gift and to recognize who has it is the parish assembly. Whenever a pastor calls a parish town hall meeting, he invites an outpouring of gifts. Through these meetings, people are in a better position to understand their own gifts and what the pastoral council ministry requires. Then they can see whether participating in the council is their vocation and whether other people see their gifts as well.[28] By spreading this discernment out over a number of meetings, participants can get to know one another. They can gauge one another's spirituality and commitment. And finally they can make a decision, either by discernment or by nomination and election, about who should be on the council.[29]

To be sure, this process is less "open" than a parish-wide election, at least in the sense that fewer people are involved in the final decision. But the involved will have gotten to know the pastoral council's purpose. They will have learned about their own gifts. And they will have had a chance to measure what other interested people might bring to the council.

In this section, I have defined the council ministry as "pastoral planning which discerns practical wisdom through the gift of dialogue." This definition builds on my criticism of council literature.

Pastoral planning is a more appropriate task for councils than coordination. Practical wisdom, not the replacement of clerical by lay leadership, is what pastors ought to seek from their councils. Those with a gift for dialogue make better councilors than those who merely reflect the parish's demographic profile. My definition of the ministry has an underlying vision, just as do the alternatives I have criticized. What is the relation between my vision and other competing visions for the council ministry?

A Synthesis of Visions

The pastor who wishes to establish or renew a pastoral council can benefit greatly from the American church's thirty years of experience with councils. That experience has sprung from efforts to embody different visions of coresponsibility in the church. In this chapter, we have identified six visions of the pastoral council. The council has been seen as an instrument for:

— coordinating lay involvement in ministry,
— pastoral planning,
— sharing leadership with the laity,
— developing a consensus,
— representing parish constituencies,
— identifying and using the gift of wisdom.

The visions have been presented as competitors. The coordination of lay ministry competes for the council's time with pastoral planning. A council for sharing leadership with the laity is in tension with another council whose pastor initiates activity and builds consensus. The council which views itself as the parish representative differs from the council whose members discern the gift of wisdom. We must admit: each of the visions which underlie these councils is important.

But given a choice, I would say that pastoral planning is a better task for a council than coordinating ministries. Coordination is important, but it is not the council's main task. Leave coordination, I would say, to the ministries themselves. Let the parish secretary handle the coordination of parish resources and facilities.

Give councilors a chance to look at the future they want for the parish.

About leadership, I would say to the pastor: exercise *your* leadership in the council. Share it with your councilors, but remember that lay leaders have their own spheres of influence. Let them exercise leadership in their own ministries. Pastoral governance is primarily the pastor's. The council exists to advise him on those matters about which he needs advice, such as clarifying the parish mission, its needs, and pastoral plan. The council may well deliberate how the parish can develop lay Christian leaders, but the council is not a lay leader "supplement" to the pastor. In the council, the pastor is the main leader, the Socrates who knows that he does not know all.

My final words to the pastor are: surround yourself with councilors whom the parish acknowledges to be good at reflection and planning. Attracting qualified people to the council is better than achieving a representative demographic profile. Representation is not unimportant—pastors need to know what parishioners are thinking. But a "representative" council may well reproduce in meetings the tensions one finds in the community, and bring dialogue to a halt. When given a choice, attract members whose primary allegiance and whose gift is the search for practical wisdom.

The underlying conciliar visions of coordinating ministries, promoting lay leadership, and representing parishioners are all important. But they should be subordinate, in the council, to pastoral planning, developing consensus about the parish mission, and calling forth the gift of wisdom.

Notes

[1] William J. Rademacher with Marliss Rogers, *The New Practical Guide for Parish Councils* (Mystic: Twenty-Third Publications, 1988), p. 23.

[2] Thomas Sweetser and Carol Holden, *Leadership in a Successful Parish* (San Francisco: Harper, 1987), p. 124.

[3] Loughlan Sofield and Brenda Hermann, *Developing the Parish as a Community of Service* (New York: Le Jacq Publishing, 1984), p. 13.

[4] William Bausch, *The Hands-On Parish* (Mystic, Connecticut: Twenty-Third Publishers, 1989), p. 89.

[5] Mary Benet McKinney, *Sharing Wisdom: A Process for Group Decision Making* (Allen, Texas: Tabor Publishing, 1987) pp. 48–49.

[6] Rademacher and Rogers, op. cit., pp. 77–78.

[7] Robert R. Newsome, *The Ministering Parish: Methods and Procedures for Pastoral Organization* (New York and Ramsey: Paulist Press, 1982), pp. 63, 80–81. Now out of print.

[8] Robert G. Howes, *Creating an Effective Parish Pastoral Council* (Collegeville: Liturgical Press, 1991), pp. 59–62.

[9] Examples are the guidelines by Baltimore (1988), Brownsville (1989), Cleveland (1990), Milwaukee (1991), and Los Angeles (1991).

[10] McKinney, op. cit., pp. 79–81.

[11] "Council of ministries" is the phrase of Thomas Sweetser and Carol Holden, op. cit., p. 126.

[12] Mark F. Fischer, "Should Your Council Have Committees?" *Today's Parish* (Jan. 1992): 15–17.

[13] Pastoral planning is the main task of the council according to Newsome, op. cit., pp. 80–81. Pastoral planning for parish renewal is the recommendation of Sofield and Hermann, op. cit.

[14] Rademacher and Rogers, op. cit., pp. 75–78.

[15] Mark F. Fischer, "What Gives Father the "Right'?" *Today's Parish* (April/May, 1992): 19–21.

[16] This is the viewpoint of Robert Howes (op. cit.). It is also implicit in the work of Peter Kim, who wants to shift the focus of councils away from maintenance ministries and toward a clarification of the parish's mission. See Peter Kim Se-Mang, *Parish Councils on Mission: Coresponsibility and Authority among Pastors and Parishioners* (Kuala Lumpur, Malaysia: Benih Publisher, 1991), esp. pp. 29–32.

[17] Bertram J. Griffin, "Diocesan Church Structures," in *Code, Community, Ministry: Selected Studies for the Parish Minister Introducing the Revised Code of Canon Law,* ed. James H. Provost (Washington, D.C.: Canon Law Society of America, 1983), p. 62.

[18] Mark F. Fischer, "Against 'Representation,' " *Today's Parish* (Sept., 1992): 23–26.

[19] This is the recommendation of McKinney, op. cit., pp. 79-81.

[20] Newsome, op. cit., pp. 80–81. Mark F. Fischer, "How Should Councils Spend Their Time?" *Today's Parish* (Part One: Sept. 1991): 20–22; (Part Two: Oct. 1991): 18–20.

[21] Loughlan Sofield and Brenda Hermann (op. cit.) argue that the council can facilitate parish renewal; and Robert G. Howes (op. cit.) stresses the need to challenge the council with a worthwhile task.

[22] This is the "management by objectives" pioneered by Peter F. Drucker in *The Practice of Management* (New York: Harper and Row, 1964) and the concept of motivation as developed by Frederick Herzberg, *Work and the Nature of Man* (New York: World Publishing, 1966). Their views are summarized in Paul Hersey and Kenneth H. Blanchard, *Management of Organizational Behavior: Utilizing Human Resources,* Sixth Edition (Englewood Cliffs, NJ: Prentice Hall, 1993), pp. 69–74, 155–157.

[23] Mark F. Fischer, "When Should a Pastor *Not* Consult the Council?" *Today's Parish* (March 1992): 18–20.

[24] *Nicomachean Ethics,* Book VI, chapter 8. This is discussed in Mark F. Fischer, "Are Pastoral Councils Competent?" *Today's Parish* (Nov./Dec. 1990): 15–16.

[25] This is the point of Peter Kim, op. cit.

[26] Mark F. Fischer, "Where Does the Pastor Fit In?" *Today's Parish* (Nov./Dec. 1991): 13–15.

[27] Mark F. Fischer, "Parish Councilors: Made or Born?" *Today's Parish* (Nov./Dec. 1993).

[28] This is the "biographical" dimension of pastoral councils, i.e., the way they relate to the life of the council member. See Klemens Schaupp, *Der Pfarrgemeinderat: eine qualitative Interview-Analyse zum Thema "Biographie und Institution"* (Innsbruck: Tyrolia Verlag, 1989, pp. 162 ff. Discussed in Mark F. Fischer, "What's More Important—Process or Product?" *Today's Parish* (Jan., 1993): 21–23.

[29] McKinney, op. cit.

A Pastor's View of How a Parish Pastoral Council Should Work

by Msgr. John F. Murphy

This chapter attempts to give an insider's view on how a parish can or should live with the new structures of our times, specifically parish pastoral councils. My experience as pastor of a suburban parish with a school is not unique. Throughout the country priests and people are trying to fit new concepts into the old wineskins of existing parish life and practice. My reflections may help others to reflect and to plan more effective ways of bringing about the vibrant faith communities our post-Vatican II parishes are called to be.

I have no intention of minimizing the wonderful things achieved in earlier parish forms. We are a strong church in the United States because of the priests and parishioners who have gone before us.

However, we are now in a new period of the church's pilgrimage and this period has been defined by the action of the Holy Spirit on the fathers of the council. Vatican II called us to a new vision of church and a new view of how we are to relate to the world. The parish becomes central to a new vision, because it is where we people live, where we experience what it means to be Catholic.

The call to all Catholics to share actively in the life of the church has resulted in new forms and structures to accomplish that. Chief among them are the councils and committees through which parishioners can work collaboratively with their pastors. I want to reflect on what the pastoral council does and, especially, how it interacts with other players on the parish scene: the pastor, the staff, other committees and groups, and indeed the whole parish.

The Players

Before considering the council, I want to remark on those whose attitudes and practices help or hinder the development of a parish community in which priest and people can work together to achieve this new vision of church.

The Pastor

I doubt if lay people give much thought to what has happened in our lifetime to the role of the parish priest. The one trained before Vatican II was schooled quite deliberately to be "in charge" of the parish. He would spend some years as an assistant, following the dictates of another, and then he would realize his dream and become a *pastor,* responsible only to God and bishop (not always in that order). Everyone else would be responsible to him.

The system often worked quite well. He was not educated to be a dictator, but a good and responsible priest who would do his duty which meant "run the parish." The failure or success rate followed the curve of human nature. Most of us can look back fondly on the men who played such large roles in our religious lives.

Vatican II and the innovations introduced after it produced a monumental change in the role of the priest as leader in the parish. Old practices and expectations yielded to new forms of parish life. I shall not belabor the point, but we cannot fully understand what happens in our parish life without acknowledging that the changes have hit the priest harder than the people.

The more recently ordained priest has been educated according to a different manual of "Pastor Do's and Don'ts." The problem he can experience is simply that his preparation hasn't included the management or leadership skills that go with leading a parish today. Letting go of a past tradition where the pastor ruled in the parish, some of today's priests may lack the confidence and the ability to take up the new, firm, visionary, skilled leadership demanded by our times and, remembering our focus, the new structures of parish life.

The care and feeding of the pastor is essential to achieving the vision. The affection, love and support of the people to whom he is sent will help him to fulfill his challenging role.

The People

When we theorize and plan for the renewed parish, we better think long and hard about the parishioners. What has transpired in the Catholic Church since Vatican II has changed their understanding and their practice about what it is to be Catholic. For many, the changes have been liberating and exhilarating; others have found those same changes threatening and troubling. If anything is sure, it is that we cannot glibly say "the parish feels . . . ," "the parish thinks . . . ," "the parish wants . . . ." Catholic people in a typical parish are all over the spectrum in their attitudes and their expectations of what it means to be Catholic and what they want (or do not want) from their parish.

This has to be remembered by both priest and other leaders within the parish. We take pride as Catholics in referring to ourselves as "Here comes everybody." Precisely because that is true, the leadership has to be mindful of the needs, the wants, and the biases of young and old, male and female, those who want to be renewed and those who prefer to be left alone.

The Parish Pastoral Council

The pastoral council is a new structure designed to help the parishioners participate actively in the life of their parish. Most Catholics would say, when asked, that they want to "participate" in their parish, but they mean different things by their answers. Some are content to be informed, others want their opinions heard; some want to share leadership, still others want to vote up or down on all parish issues.

The parish pastoral council is a unique, collaborative body. It does not have the power of vote or veto, but it is called to share with the pastor in determining all the important matters that affect the life of the faith community. It is to be a representative group of serious, faith-filled Christian men and women who try to lead their

parish into becoming what a community of twentieth-century baptized people is supposed to be!

To achieve its goal in the parish effectively, the council has to
be a body which visions, plans, oversees, coordinates, communicates and evaluates.

The Council Envisions

The first thing for a council to get is a *vision* of church. This is
the key to their ministry. Otherwise, a council becomes at best a
committee which concerns itself with meddling in the administration of a parish plant.

The accomplishments of Vatican II are centered on its vision
of what Christ's church is called to be at this moment of its history.
Lumen Gentium and *Gaudium et Spes* contain the vision of the
church in our times. It is a splendid, profound, energizing vision. A
chief responsibility of the pastor is to help the people acquire this
vision of the church, so that they can then determine what is the
mission of their own part of the church, their parish.

Grasping this vision is a challenging job. It requires reading
and prayer, reflection and learning, often from outside sources.
Dioceses may need to provide resource persons to help individual
parishes deepen their theological understanding of the vision.
Skilled process people can also guide pastoral councils to use their
own experience and insights in the development of the parish's
mission.

The Council Plans

Every pastor knows that the best way to engage all the members of a group is to ask them what color to paint the church or
whether the dress code can be changed in the school. The tempta-
tion faced by every council, and indeed, every parish committee, is
to do the administrative tasks that belong to the pastor or some
staff member. The first responsibility of the parish council is to
plan. It looks to the future. It determines priorities and works to
achieve them.

Determining those priorities and how they relate to the mission of this parish as understood by its members usually means the

council has to utilize some method of need assessment. Parish surveys and opinion polls are all part of helping to make the determination of where parish emphasis, energy, and money are to go. For example, if the council rightly concludes that good Sunday liturgy has the highest priority among all the parishioners, and the present music program is deficient, does not increased funding for music outrank improvements on the gym?

Pastoral planning, as we know it today, is a new phenomenon in the average parish. It is not a new concept, but planning in the past often did not use the concepts and methodologies developed by modern management science. Management science helps people with planning and analysis in new and systematic ways. Managers were assisted in studying the "environment" facing the company or organization. They clarified the goals they wished to reach, studied the markets open to them, examined weaknesses and strengths in their positions, laid out options, identified resources, estimated costs, made decisions, and then designed mechanisms to evaluate what they had done.

The foregoing does not describe *pastoral planning,* but it indicates some of the elements that should go into it. The two most important elements for pastoral planning are, as we have seen, the *mission* and the *participants.* This means, simply, 1) theological reflection done by 2) the church (here read parish).

If the council does its task well, the whole parish membership will find itself involved in determining what it means to be church and what that requires by way of parish planning. The more deeply we explore Christ's call to his people, the more clearly the parish will see that preoccupation with buildings (even important ones such as churches and schools) must take second place to finding what God's will is for this community of faith.

Vision describes the ideal parish community; *planning* enables the council to lead the parish to it.

The Council Oversees

The council is called to oversee, but not to meddle! The pastor and his staff administer the policies which are initiated or approved by the council. Not all policies need to come before committees or councils. The principle of subsidiarity dictates they should be handled at the most appropriate level. However, the council needs to be satisfied with parish policies and with their administration. They exercise an oversight role with the pastor, not having to look at everything, but able to exercise their leadership in policy formation where it is needed, and to hold "doers" accountable for adhering to those policies.

A typical council will have a number of standing and special committees assigned specific tasks such as worship or Christian formation or family life. The council helps the committees to set their description and agenda, then gives them the room to do their jobs. Reporting procedures should be clear and crisp. Details should be kept to a minimum at council level. The council oversees by engaging its committees in discussing their year's work in advance and then in getting reports and evaluating accomplishments at year's end.

Having spent the majority of my life in some form of management, I value highly the council's oversight function. Here is where the representatives of the parish have a share in the total responsibility for the parish. Pastors come and go. The parishioners should see themselves collectively as the enduring community. It is to their representatives that they give their powers of oversight of that community. To me, the concept of oversight carries two parts: one, no part of the parish's life should be outside the purview of the council; two, the council oversees everything with the pastor, but oversight does not mean getting mired down in details or in interfering with those who have specific responsibilities.

The Council Coordinates

I emphasize the coordinating role of council in a parish because I think it is called to keep projects and people related. Often this requires diplomacy and sensitivity to the feelings and opinions of others. What comes to mind are the groups which have been in the parish for generations. Some have to do with athletic or recreational programs for youth or social activities of older parishioners. The pastor and the council have to make clear to the parish the oversight and coordinating role they fill, keeping everything connected to the vision and mission. But a deft hand is clearly called for there. As pastor I was totally committed to this function of the council, but I have to admit that at times this didn't work as well as I would have liked. For the council to invite all groups to meet with them at the beginning and end of the year to hear their plans and receive their reports is a coordinating aspect of visioning and overseeing and could also be a way of acknowledging the work they do within the parish. Coordination therefore does not mean playing peace-maker or arbitrator during the course of the year whenever scheduling problems or similar "operational" glitches occur.

The Pastoral Council and the Finance Council

Since the finance council not only has a special function in church law, but also is closely involved with parish life, I want to call special attention to its relation to the pastoral council. Not everyone may know that the pastor *has* to have a finance council, while it is only recommended that he have a pastoral council! I find this an unfortunate distinction as it seems to imply that finances are of more importance than pastoral matters. It was of concern to me for another reason. I didn't want two centers of "power" in the parish. I shared this concern quite openly with both councils and we agreed that the pastoral council would be asked to give their endorsement to all major actions of the finance council, particularly the budget and the reception of the annual report. I stated that I would withhold my pastoral endorsement of these major issues until they had passed both bodies. I think being candid about my reasons helped; also, there were no pending actions when I announced my position.

The Pastoral Council and the Stewardship Program

Stewardship is a major issue for every parish, whether one wishes to look at it in its fullest dimensions as some stewardship programs do and as the bishops' 1992 statement on discipleship has done, or in the narrower sense of an offertory enhancement program.

The pastoral council cannot ignore stewardship because it is the way we act as disciples. From the point of view of funding itself, planners (pastoral council) cannot ignore the fiscal implications of their plans. The leadership which assumes responsibility for determining the direction of the parish and its various priorities cannot duck the obligations of coming to grips with how programs and plans will be paid for.

The concept of stewardship is very embracing. It is critical to the life of the parish. Ongoing studies treat of the problems we are having as Catholic Americans sharing our wealth with the church. I do not know the answers to our problems, but I know we cannot fund what we say we want as parishioners with so many registered Catholics sharing so little of their income. I think the stewardship responsibility should be separated from the primary role of the finance council, although it could be a subcommittee reporting to the finance council. I think the finance council has the task of managing the parish's funds, not in acquiring them. Certainly, I should add, not in deciding how they are to be spent, either!

A stewardship committee should not only monitor parish giving programs and assume responsibility for bringing such matters continually to the attention of the parishioners. I think they should serve somewhat as the "conscience" of both pastoral council and the parish in general in calling their fellow parishioners to live their lives as true disciples of Christ, sharing with others as a gift all that they have themselves received as a gift: their life and talents, their time, and their treasure.

The Council Communicates

One way to judge the success of a pastoral council is to see how well it communicates with the parish. It is easy for the uninformed parishioner to assert that he is on the "outside" and that he/she has nothing to say about what is going on. I happen to think it is almost always incorrect to think some few parishioners are trying to do a power grab and control the parish! Most parish leaders would do anything to be joined in their work by others, and would be very happy to put time limits on their periods of service.

Misunderstandings develop when things are not adequately communicated. Many people, not Catholic, have wildly inaccurate opinions about the church because we are often poor communicators (*evangelizers* is the more proper word) of the Good News. At the parish level, communicating and reporting should have high priority among council tasks. The council should budget an adequate amount for this purpose, either for mailings direct to parishioners' homes and/or for parish newsletters/newspapers.

There are certain matters that both pastoral and finance councils should see are communicated well. First, the pastoral council should clearly state what its annual program and objectives will be. At year's end it should give a concise report on how it has achieved those goals. The finance council should send out good, understandable reports which do not require an experienced accountant to interpret or so broadly stated that they are meaningless for all practical purposes. Charts and graphs make figures more meaningful. Every home receives many clear financial reports in the mailbox. Seldom are there attractive and readable reports from the parish!

There are other means than the written word to communicate the work of parish leadership. Some parishes find it is effective to have a council spokesperson give short, periodic reports in the announcement slot at the weekend liturgies. Occasional open "town hall" type meetings are another way of making reports and, also, of fielding questions and hearing comments.

We sometimes allow our reporting procedures to be meager, because we hear little feedback. That's not always a valid measure of success. Look at how few letter writers there are to newspapers when thousands are reading, either agreeing or disagreeing but not getting around to writing a letter! I think the bottom line should be that there just can't be enough communication on all parish affairs. Do them well and do them often!

The Council Evaluates

The primary function of the pastoral council is to plan, and the process of planning is incomplete without arranging for evaluation.

We are often inclined to skip it or do it carelessly. When done well, it helps us to put a finish to completed work; it also suggests how the next cycle of planning can be improved on.

Here again, a council might be assisted by a "process person." There are a lot of these people around now who have skills to make this part of the council's work go smoothly. A note in the parish bulletin could uncover a parishioner who could use those skills as part of the contribution of time and talent.

Conclusion

I have an unwritten essay in my mind about how today's pastor needs to see meetings as his modern ministry. It won't be a popular best seller, but it will express a reality in today's church. Often I hear priests regretting the many meetings they must attend, almost as though they didn't count as legitimate work: "Individual counseling is priestly work, visiting the sick is priestly work; going to meetings is not!"

I submit that the reality of parish life today is that the meetings of and with parishioners are a major way the church's work is done. How can parishioners participate in their ownership of the church and its mission unless they are given opportunities and challenges to join with their pastor in discovering the vision, articulating the parish's mission, working with fellow parishioners to plan for and bring about the reign of God?

This chapter is my testimony to the importance of parish pastoral councils. I hope my experience and observations are of some help to those who want to start a pastoral council or improve its functioning within the parish.

Choosing Pastoral Council Members

by Mary Kay Bailey, OP

Before we can speak in a meaningful way about selecting members for a parish pastoral council, it is important to remind ourselves of our basic vision of church, for a council functions as a structure within the overall structure of the Roman Catholic Church, and the mission of the council is to develop and support the mission of the church.

Vatican II Image of the Church

Below is an important paragraph taken from the letter of Pope John Paul II in which he gave the revised Code of Canon Law to the church in 1983. This apostolic constitution can be found in the front of each edition of the revised code. The copy I prepared for this article is set not in paragraph form, but in list form so that one can see the six major points more easily.

Among the elements which characterize the true and genuine image of the Church we should emphasize especially the following:

- the doctrine in which the Church is presented as the People of God (cf. dogmatic constitution *Lumen Gentium*, chapter 2), and

- hierarchical authority as serving (ibid., chapter 3)

- the doctrine in which the church is seen as a "communion" and which therefore determines the relations which are to exist between the particular churches and the universal church, and between collegiality and primacy,

• likewise the doctrine according to which all the members of the People of God, in the way suited to each of them, participate in the threefold priestly, prophetic and kingly office of Christ,

• to which doctrine is also linked that which concerns the duties and rights of the faithful and particularly the laity; and

• finally, the Church is to commit to ecumenism.[1]

The first point is very familiar: the church as the people of God. It unites all of the members and each of the members: laity, ordained, vowed women and men. Each person has a place and a role but it is all of these together which make up the church, the people of God.

As with any human structure there are different roles and responsibilities within the church. Points two through five describe something about them.

Hierarchical authority is for service, not for control. The one in a position of authority is to shepherd, to take care of, those people to whom the person is responsible and accountable. The leader leads, that is, supports and draws out, the people in the group. The leader does not control by command or force. As Archbishop Patrick F. Flores of San Antonio says, "I am the minister to the ministers."

In working with groups of people within the church, I find that most people think that the third point is the "heart of the matter." How are members of the church being called to relate to one another today? They are called to be in "communion": the bishops and the pope together, not one against or over the other: dioceses and the universal church together, not apart or individual. That is the way in which Christians are to relate to one another, not only as individuals and within families, but also within and among parishes, within and among church organizations. All are called to be in "communion."

The fourth point says that, in this "communion," each person is to participate in the threefold priestly, prophetic and kingly office of Christ. As a child I heard adults talking about the three things one had to do to be a member of the church in good standing: "pray, pay and obey." And I experienced in my young adult life that I was only asked to be passive, to be a recipient. Oh, yes, I was sometimes asked to do things, like, well, raffle tickets, donate items for a festival booth or help clean up the hall after some activity.

Look at the difference now! Each member is called to be responsible in some way for the life of the church: priestly—to actively support the prayer and worship of the parish; prophetic—to actively learn about one's faith, and then to evangelize and to teach; kingly—to serve the needs of others within the church, the community and the world. All of these responsibilities flow from baptism which make an individual a member of the body of Christ, the people of God. As with all human memberships, each person therefore becomes responsible for the life and the health of the group.

Point five highlights that in the revised code there is a naming of the duties and rights of the faithful and in particular of the laity. For a long time the church has noted the duties and the rights of the ordained and the vowed religious. Now the laity are specifically included!

We are not going to take the time to review those lists here, but I encourage you to ask your pastor or director of religious education to show you the part of the code which has those paragraphs. When you do, please don't limit yourself—look at the duties as well as the rights.

The final point which Pope John Paul II notes is interesting and, at first glance, different than the first five. The church is to commit to ecumenism, that is, we are to pray and work for the day in which all Christian churches will be united as one.

I don't know what the exact numbers are, but I do know that

in the United States we have more than 250 different Christian sects. Our scriptures proclaim, "One Lord, one faith, one baptism," but others see division among us as followers of Jesus.

Point six takes us back to point one: the church, the assembly, is the people of God. That is the church that all of its members are called to help build.

A Call to Ministry

It is within the kind of church which has just been described that parish pastoral councils exist. Because church members are called to a new way of looking, seeing—all have a new way of being church as Pope Paul VI said—leadership groups like councils are viewed in a new way.

It is not my task within this chapter to describe the role of a parish pastoral council as such. Other presentations in this book have addressed that topic. I do want to reemphasize, however, that the mission of the council is to develop and support the mission of the church. With that said it is time to begin looking at a method for obtaining members for such a group.

With a basic understanding of church as described in the revised Code of Canon Law—which only reflects the teachings of the Second Vatican Council —I believe one can say that the call to be a pastoral council member is a call to ministry within the church. The method for selecting members which will be reviewed here is based, therefore, on the idea of *call* rather than on the idea of winning an election.

The call to ministry implies: first, the church has a need; second, a given person has the skill, time and energy to meet the need; third, someone representing the church affirms that the given person is "someone for the job," and calls that individual to ministry.

Following the steps named, a process for selecting pastoral council members would begin with informing and educating parishioners about the role and functions of the council. This can be done with announcements, bulletin articles, and presentations at masses. If people of your parish will come to sessions at other times, a series of presentations could be given.

A part of the education phase is to name some of the criteria by which a person can evaluate if he or she has the gifts necessary for serving in this ministry. During the next step, a recommendation process, these criteria are listed in writing (some are to be found later in this chapter) and become the introduction to a simple form which is made available to as many parishioners as possible for a two to three week period.

The recommendation form reads, "I suggest that _____ be considered as a possible member of our Parish Pastoral Council because _____," leaving two of three lines for the reasons to be named. It is common for the name and telephone number of the person making the recommendation to be requested. "Why?" you ask.

In a large parish someone could be suggested whom no one on the staff or present council knows, and this provides a way to contact the individual through the person who is doing the recommending. Also, in general, information received from people willing to be identified is said to be more reliable than information given by someone unknown.

After the deadline for submitting recommendations has been reached, the pastor meets with members of his staff and/or the pastoral council. They divide up the recommendation forms among them and begin calling the recommended people by phone.

"Hello, _____. This is _____, a present member of the pastoral council. You have been recommended as a possible new member of the council. I am phoning to congratulate you and to tell you what the next steps will be if you're interested in at least finding out more about this ministry."

If the person says, "Thank you for calling. I am honored, but I don't think that job is for me," or any similar idea, you simply say, "Thank you." Ask for prayer for the parish, hang up and proceed to the next phone call.

If the person sounds interested, you keep on talking: "We will be having (give the number of sessions, dates, times and location) to learn in more detail about the role and functions of a pastoral council in the church today. You will also have the chance to learn more about the qualities and skills that it is helpful for a council member to have. Remember that no one person has them all but it is good for the council as a whole to have as many as possible. When the learning sessions have been completed, there will be a discernment process among those remaining in the process to determine who is being called to serve on the council at this time in the parish's history.

"We'd like to give you the chance to think about this if you need the time. Simply phone (the pastor or whoever is delegated) to tell him/her if you will participate in the process or not; we ask you to contact him/her by (date). Please know that I will be praying for you. Thank you for considering this invitation to serve our community in this way."

The content of the learning sessions to which potential members are invited is greatly influenced by one's diocesan guidelines for a parish pastoral council. Some parishes have four to six sessions of two hours each; others have two four-hour sessions, still others one six-hour session, etc. The number depends upon what one wants to cover, the meeting patterns of the parishioners and the availability of presenters and facilities.

For the purpose only of this chapter, a broad explanation of a parish pastoral council is included here. (This is not a definition for debate but simply a statement upon which to illustrate a selection of members process.) The first sentence describes its role and the second with three parts names its primary functions in broad categories.

A parish pastoral council is a consultative body to the pastor, composed of members of the parish staff and members of the parish, which promotes pastoral action through reflection and planning.

The pastoral council helps the parish community to:
1) be in touch with its identity and its values,
2) articulate its vision/mission,
3) identify achievable goals.

Criteria for Membership

A beginning list of criteria for membership on the pastoral council described and with the church with the aforementioned characteristics is offered below. To be able to serve on the council a person needs the attitudes and at least some of the skills listed—an openness to developing the other skills.

Criteria

Attitudes
- a registered and participating member of the faith community, including regular participation in the Sunday worship
- an ability to listen
- an ability to articulate accurately what one has heard
- a desire for spiritual growth
- an openness to study and reflection
- an eagerness to help the parish articulate its vision or direction

Skills
- an ease in working in groups
- an ability to inspire and lead others
- a willingness to delegate responsibilities
- an ability to "follow through" after making a commitment
- an ability to make decisions
- an excitement about the parish
- availability of time and focused energy

This new way of being church means that those who serve it need to learn new ways of operating—to develop new attitudes of being—to establish new ways of relating to one another. Please take time to read through the list again. Are there other attitudes, qualities, skills that need to be on the list for your parish?

Selection by Discernment

There are many different methods of discernment. Basically, however, discernment indicates that a person and the Holy Spirit agree on what the person is to do in a given situation. With regard to ministry, a third person representing the church is an integral part of the process. Although it is not the purpose of this chapter to teach the reader how to do a discernment process, the following set of questions is offered to illustrate the kind of personal reflection in which a potential council member needs to participate. The criteria to which the questions refer could be those in the list above, some prepared by the reader, or a list put together by the participants themselves after understanding more clearly what a council is and does.

Beginning My Discernment

— Using the numerals 1, 2, 3, 4, 5 (with 1 indicating the greatest strength), assign them to the five criteria which you see yourself meeting.
— Given the list of criteria, which one of these is my greatest strength? How do I use this gift?
— Given the list of criteria, which one of these is my greatest weakness? What am I doing to overcome it?
— List the church-related involvements which you NOW have:
— List the other involvements which you NOW have:
— When you say "yes" to doing a job, performing a task, attending a meeting, etc., do you do, perform, attend, etc.? Or do you not follow through on your word?
— Given your lists of church-related and other commitments, which you now have, do you see yourself having the time and focused energy to serve on the pastoral council? Would you need to give something up? If so, what? Would you do so?
— Do you have a primary leadership role in any parish group? If yes, list the ways that could help you as a member of the pastoral council—ways that could hinder you.
— Group decision making involves the question, "What is the best thing for this group at this time in its history?" Would you be able to participate in this kind of

process? . . . hearing what each one says and then
seeking the group's good? . . . letting go of your own
agenda?

— Using your answers as part of your input, what do
you think God is calling you to do regarding the
ministry of parish pastoral council?

It is good for a person to be able to name his/her greatest
strength and greatest weakness; this indicates the self-knowledge
and the ability to admit strengths and weaknesses. The remaining
directions and questions lead a person to reflect upon time, energy
and the attitude needed to participate in group decision making.
After completing this list of questions in writing, a person would
be in a better position to answer the final question.

If this information is discussed with another person or in a
group, an individual shares the answers orally but does not turn the
paper over to someone else to read. Knowing that the written
responses will not be read by anyone else helps the person writing
to be more honest with self.

After all the individuals come to know if they are being called
to pastoral council ministry, one often has more people ready to
serve than there are vacant positions. Again, there are many different methods used to arrive at the number of people needed.

The pastor might decide to draw names by lot. Names are
placed on individual slips of paper, face down, on a table. Then a
few names are drawn at each of the weekend masses. Persons
whose names are drawn serve on the council and the remaining
persons are in an available pool in case a replacement is needed for
someone who must resign.

Another way to select the members is to have an open dialogue among all those who feel themselves called to this ministry.
They would take turns naming the strengths and weaknesses of
each person; then each person would list the required number of
persons he/she heard as being the most affirmed. The lists are then
turned upward on a table and scanned by everyone passing by the
table. After those participating have scanned the list, the question
is asked, "Whom do we see as having been chosen?"

Usually it is very apparent who has been named and often it is the full number needed. If only a few persons are evidently identified on this first round, the process is repeated until the number of persons needed is obtained. (This is a situation in which you would want a good process facilitator, preferably an "outsider," leading the group.)

Conclusion

This chapter may have raised more questions than answers. But if you have been introduced to the idea that selecting pastoral council members by a call process is more appropriate than an election and you are willing to pursue the possibility, then your reading time has been fruitful.

You might also note that this format, if adopted, can be used for all kinds of ministries, not only the parish pastoral council. My prayer is with you as you continue to look for more effective ways to select members for your pastoral council.

Note

[1] Taken from Apostolic Constitution *Sacrae Disciplinae Leges* of Pope John Paul II.

The Power in EmPOWERment

by Eileen Tabert

I have a question for you: Why do you serve on your parish pastoral council? Why do you dedicate your discretionary hours to volunteer parish leadership work?

Probably because, in one way or another, each one of us was chosen by the creator of the universe to serve in the church and to ultimately make a difference in the world. Each of us was *called* by name and chosen to this leadership role in a parish. We heard the call and we accepted it.

Now in my case I am very aware that my call was not as dramatic as the call of Moses. There was no burning bush to herald me to ministry. Mine at best was a tiny, tiny whisper . . . so tiny that many times I had to stop and say, "Are you calling me, God? Are you sure it's me you want? I have nothing very special to offer." But then I realized that God had chosen Peter and the first group of "ministers" personally—and they weren't any great shakes! Jesus was the most gifted teacher in the world, yet the apostles kept asking, "What are you talking about?" They were slow to get the message. Still Jesus had patience with them.

And I have come to believe that during my 22 years of parish council ministry Jesus has lost none of his patience—or his sense of humor—because he hasn't ever once given up on me!

And sure enough, that call that I heard, tiny whisper though it was, proved real and true. I have a place in the church today— exactly the same as your place in the church—a place of leadership.

Mentioning Moses' call to ministry reminds me of a story. When my daughters were little, they would come home from school each day to be asked the magic question, "Lisa, Kristen, what did you do in school today?" and for the next *four hours* they

71

would tell me every single thing that happened during the course of the school day, down to the minutest detail. That's how little girls are!

Now on the other hand, there's my nephew, Kevin—a seven-year-old bundle of energy. One day he stopped in after school, and I instinctively asked, "So, Kevin, what did you learn in school today?"

His answer: "Nothing."

"But Kevin, you must have learned something."

"Nope, nothing."

Now I've taken creative questioning courses for a reason. I'm not giving up easily.

"Kevin, did you have religion today?"

"Yup."

"What did you talk about?"

"Moses."

"Kevin, why don't you tell me what you learned about Moses."

"OK, Aunt Eileen," he conceded. "Well, you see, there was this guy, Moses, and he and his people lived in this place called Egypt. But they weren't happy. You know why? Because of this other guy, Pharaoh, who made them slaves. So Moses went to the Pharaoh one day and said 'You better let my people go!' Pharaoh looked at Moses and said 'Not on your life.' So Moses said to Pharaoh, 'If you don't let my people go, a lot of bad things will happen to you.' And Pharaoh said, 'Oh yeah, let's see!'

"All of a sudden, all kinds of bad things started to happen to Pharaoh, like the water went red and frogs and toads and snakes jumped out. Pharaoh yelled, 'Stop, Stop, Moses! Take your people and get out of here.' Moses said 'Great.'

"So Moses and his people packed up and went running across the desert because now they were free.

"All of a sudden one of the guys in the back of the crowd yelled out 'Hey, Moses, look!' Moses turned around—and you know what he saw? Pharaoh's whole army running toward him, with chariots and everything. Moses looked in front of him and there was this huge river. What should he do! Moses yelled, 'Quick, men, throw down the pontoon bridges.' Plop, plop, plop.

'Women and children: run across the bridge. 'Men, turn your canons around and when I give the word, you FIRE! OK!'

"Boom, boom, boom! There, Pharaoh's whole army is wiped out. Moses and his men go running across the pontoon bridge and they're in the promised land."

"Kevin," I asked, stunned. "Is that the way your teacher told you that Moses and his people got to the promised land?"

He looked at me with his seven year old wisdom and said, "Aunt Eileen, if I told you how my *teacher* said it happened, you'd never believe me!"

So, we are church leaders. We've been called to leadership on a parish level. But what does it mean to be a leader? First and foremost, it means that each of us has to give up being a "Do-er"! I want you to post a STOP sign on your mirror, tie a string around your finger, or do whatever it takes to remind yourself that you are—for this time and place in your life—a parish leader, and that fact requires that you *stop doing,* so that you can empower others to become involved through your leadership.

The purpose of this chapter is to offer some suggestions on ways to empower others to "do." Let's use the acronym R-A-T-E-D as a teaching tool.

R is for Recruit

To stop doing and start leading you have first to learn good recruitment skills. You can't be part of a leadership team which envisions the direction of your parish . . . your committee . . . your particular ministry . . . if you don't have people to ultimately implement the vision.

There is one phrase you should remember when considering a recruitment effort: "Be a joyful recruiter." Nobody wants to join a doleful team. I rehearse every time I recruit. Really, I rehearse the whole conversation in front of a mirror. If I can't convince the person staring out at me to say "yes," there's no way that I will successfully sell the project to anyone else.

Some people think that it's hard to recruit face-to-face for two reasons:

— that type of recruiting puts people on the spot;
— it hurts when people turn you down.

But remember this. In the major leagues, if you bat .400 you are assured the batting crown. So why pressure yourself into batting 1.000 when you recruit? The point is to practice good recruiting. Learn by trying. Your average will consistently improve.

The two worst places to recruit are in the church lobby after mass on Sunday and at the supermarket. Why? Because it's viewed by the potential volunteer as spur-of-the-moment. Don't recruit casually. When I'm in the supermarket and someone says, "Boy, Eileen, am I glad that I ran into you! I've been meaning to call you regarding this new project that I'm working on . . . ," that person has immediately lost me. When you recruit, do it intentionally, not casually.

There is nothing you do as a leader that is more important than recruiting. Give the person you are attempting to recruit a feeling of that importance. If you see the individual at Sunday mass, light conversation is in order, followed two days later by your "recruitment call." It's very powerful—especially when a committee chairperson, parish council president or pastor, calls to say, "Hi, Tony, this is Father Jay. Is Kathy home? I'd like to talk to her about a special project." Immediately, the job takes on a deeper importance.

Never recruit by saying, "We've got a committee that's going to look at a new library for the school. We want you to be on it." Before you approach someone, make sure you know why you're asking that particular person. What gift is he/she going to bring to the project? Make that clear right up front.

"Jeanne, you seem to have great love for the school. We know you are involved in the Township Library's Literacy Program, and thought you might be familiar with some book publishers who could help us with plans for our proposed school library. When we were talking about people for this committee, your name was the first one to surface. Your input would be great!"

Have the parameters of the job at your fingertips. "We hope to be getting together every other Thursday through March and April, for a total of nine meetings. At the end of that time we hope to have a plan ready to present to the parish pastoral council and school board."

Be a joyful recruiter. Do your homework before attempting to recruit. Share with a potential volunteer the parameters of the task, the particular reason that you want him/her as part of the project, and the proposed timeline. Get the *right person* for the right job—and you're term as a parish leader will be most productive, energizing, and yes, even fun!

"A" for Affirm

From your position as leader, you should be very aware of the importance of the first meeting a volunteer attends, for it is here that you have the opportunity to welcome that person with quality. There is nothing more frustrating to me than to be present at a pastoral council meeting, where the chairperson announces, "I want to introduce our two new members, Bill Farrell and Larry Lynch. Welcome to both of you . . . and now on to business."

In the first place, it should not be taken for granted that Bill and Larry know all of the members of the pastoral council, or that all present know them—even if they have lived in the parish for eons! Take the time to introduce with quality. Find out as much about new members as you can. Share with the group the gifts that a new member will bring to the team. This applies to any parish group—whether a committee, a task force, or a council.

You will never have a problem picking out the newest members of a group. They are the ones who *come on time* to that first meeting! For some reason, when we schedule church meetings for eight o'clock, we are still strolling in at ten after eight. What are we teaching new members? Come ten minutes late to the next meeting! If you really want to respect the gift of discretionary time that is offered by every member of the group, always start your meetings on time.

Here's another way you can affirm new members of the pastoral council. Invite them as members of the parish leadership body to dinner at the rectory—followed by a tour of the parish facilities. Don't presume that they know all about the parish physical plant. It is through the walk through that asbestos problems or potential roof replacement will be pointed out. That sharing of ownership is part of affirmation. The new member, driving home after that first meeting, should feel very much a valued part of the leadership team.

That's your job—to make sure they believe that, if absent at the next meeting, *they will be missed.* Now that's affirmation.

"T" for Training

Membership in a particular group does not bring with it an immediate acquisition of knowledge. I remember when I was first asked to be a lector, twenty years ago. My answer: "No way. I'm not very good at public speaking." My pastor, a most persuasive individual, persisted . . . and I finally relented. Driving home I had a little talk with God: "Well I said 'yes'—now what?" I some-how had this hope that I would wake up the following Sunday morning with a well-trained tongue, effortlessly able to proclaim 'seraph serpents and scorpions' without stuttering . . . but that didn't happen.

I lectored at the 6:30 am mass each Sunday for one full year, until I thought I had acquired enough ability to handle the chal-lenge of a more well-attended mass.

Yet we put people on a parish council, expecting them to miraculously know everything there is to know about parish leader-ship roles and responsibilities.

Book II of the new Code of Canon Law is entitled "The People of God," and contains Canon 231 which states:

Lay persons who are pledged to the special service of the Church, whether permanently or for a time, have a duty to acquire the appropriate formation which their role de-mands, so that they may conscientiously, earnestly and diligently fulfill this role.

While parish councils are not mandated by canon law, *training* for volunteers who serve the church *is.* Think about it.

I believe annual retreats should be a precondition for serving in a leadership role on a council. I know some will say, "Eileen, be realistic! Who's got the time?" Well, if I've been called to give three —or two or six—years of my life to the church in a leadership position, then part of that time should be spent in formation and training for the work that I have agreed to undertake.

As parish councilors, one of the best investments we can make of our time is sharing in this annual retreat day. After all, we are not called to be a group of decision makers who now-and-then prays. We are called to be prayerful, spiritual people who now-and-then make decisions. If skills in parish planning, visioning, implementing are to happen, then the climate of a day of retreat provides the essential spiritual underpinning. Jesus, the greatest teacher, found it necessary to take his little band of leaders away occasionally for renewal, reflection and refreshment. Let us imitate the Master. We owe that much to ourselves.

One of my favorite corporate executives is Frederick Crawford, the salty CEO of TRW Enterprises, now a huge, sprawling, Fortune 500 company. Mr. Crawford once said that there were only two organizations in the United States that were able to succeed in spite of their poor leadership qualities: the U S Army and the Roman Catholic Church.

When I first heard the quote, it really bothered me. But the more I thought about it, the more I realized he had a point. For the most part, we do not invest time and/or treasure in training our parish leaders to be optimally effective. We in parish life are the most meeting-intense people on the planet. Yet, what of the quality of our meetings? Some have estimated that as many as half of the attendees at these meetings leave frustrated, discouraged, hurt or angry.

Evidence of this can be found in your church parking lot after a parish meeting. Anyone who leaves the gathering with feelings of frustration—anyone who is an introvert by nature and was never given the opportunity of expressing his/her ideas because extroverts are allowed to dominate the conversation—anyone who feels discouragement or anger because the certain little "inside clique" seemed to have made all of the decisions prior to the meeting . . . any and all of these good people will stand around, in small isolated clusters—even in the worst weather—and finish the meeting in the midst of parked cars. This recurring situation indicates that

we do not put enough priority into instilling good leadership qualities into our key parish people.

Forbes magazine mentioned some time ago that the annual bill
paid by corporate America to train upper and middle management
had exceeded seven hundred million dollars per year. I can believe
that because every single day of the week I am inundated with
invitations to attend seminars geared toward making me a better
manager/leader. Workshops are offered on how to cope with
stress, how to dress for success, how to speak and write powerfully,
how to attain the right "look" for an office . . . you name it:
they've got a workshop for it!

The point is that companies spend a fortune on training. I
have a question for parish finance people. I'm not trying to put you
on the spot, but how much of the parish budget is allocated for
training? Does your treasury allow for the aggressive pursuit of
ministry excellence by all of your parish leaders? Treasure spent on
enhancing the time and talent gifts of leaders will come back one-
hundred-fold.

I learned about investing in training in a unique way. When
my daughter Lisa was five years old, my husband, John, decided to
give her a small allowance. To earn it, she was to do the dishes
every night. Granted today's kids don't get their hands wet when
they do the dishes—they fill the dishwasher! Well, that was Lisa's
chore.

My youngest daughter, Kristen, who was two-and-a-half at
the time, watched Lisa work for two or three nights, then announced, "Mommy, I want to do that too." Anything Lisa did
Kristen wanted to try.

"Honey, you're just a little bit too small for this job."

"But, Mommy, can't I just try?"

Have you ever tried to train a two-year-old to load a dishwasher?

That first night it took us a little over an hour. (Luckily patience is one of my strong suits.) Kristen was so excited when she
got to turn the dishwasher on!

Two nights later, we finished the loading in fifty minutes—and
by the time Kristen was three, she stacked the dishes as well as
Lisa.

Every New Year's Day, our local funeral director would supply each parish family with a calendar. My husband would sit down with Lisa and Kristen, and together they would write an "L" or a "K" for each day of the year, identifying whose turn it was to do the dishes.

What point am I trying to make? I spent approximately seven hours over the course of twelve nights teaching Kristen how to "do" dishes, and for the next fifteen years I was given a block of time each night for other uses. Training, therefore, is essential if your goal is to encourage other people to be the do-ers.

There is a little parish in Bay St. Louis, Mississippi. When the parish was four years old, the young parish council was struggling with some serious questions. What is our role? Are we a decision-making council or an advisory council? What committees do we need?

One morning the pastor was flipping through a magazine that had arrived in the mail, and he came across an advertisement for the annual convention of diocesan liturgists, which was being held that year in Chicago. He cut out the announcement and sent it to his liturgy chairperson—brand new on the job—along with a note that said, "Diane, this just caught my eye. Why don't you check it out and report at the next council meeting?"

Diane's report to the council on the following Tuesday night went something like this: "At Father Bill's suggestion, I called this National Liturgical group and asked if the conference was only for diocesan people, or were parish folks allowed to attend. I was assured that everyone was welcome. It will cost $450 for each of us if we purchase group airfare tickets for our ten liturgy committee people and share two-to-a-room accommodations. I touched base with my whole committee, and everyone would be willing to go— even if it means taking vacation or personal time from work for the four-day conference, if you, the parish council, think we can invest that much money in our committee."

The council talked about it at length, because the total cost of $4,500 was quite a substantial amount of money for a new parish to dedicate to training. In the end, the council agreed to the expenditure, and the ten liturgy committee members set out for Chicago— with an extra $500 gift from the pastor for "hospitality."

They were welcomed to the national Conference with open arms—and set about the task of learning all that was to be learned. Their contingency of ten was enough to cover every workshop in every time slot: children's choir, folk choirs, adult choirs, lectors, children's liturgies, greeters. Back in the hospitality room each night, they would sit for hours discussing the seminars they had attended that day.

They prayed together, played together, planned together, learned together. On the flight back home, their plane didn't even need fuel, that group was flying so high! Does quality training work? Well, if you're real quiet on a Sunday morning about 10:15, you'll probably hear the singing all the way from Bay St. Louis.

Do you think that little parish has a problem recruiting people for the parish council? Do you think the parish council chairpeople have a problem getting parishioners to make a commitment to volunteer? NO! For the parish has learned what the corporate world discovered long ago. They learned that an investment in quality training guarantees a committed, effective and productive leadership group.

So training is essential!

"E" for EmPOWERment

We've recruited. We've affirmed. We've trained. We've got one great leadership group there. Now they're gathered at a meeting.

I would never hold a parish council meeting without having in the middle of the table an index card on every family in my parish. *Every family.* I'd place a gold star on the cards of those who had already participated in "something" during the course of the year. And my challenge to the council would be to gold star every card, every family in the parish by the end of each year. Then and only then would we get a gold star as an empowering council.

The only way the council can achieve this goal is by spending quality time at meetings deciding how to encourage those families who do not participate in parish life to do so. People who do nothing usually have not been asked properly to do something, or they have been asked to do the wrong thing. Your job as a leadership community is to empower others by asking the right people to volunteer for the right tasks. Matchmakers, that's the ticket!

No matter which parish I visit, I hear that familiar line: "The same few people do all the work!" I find I say it to myself every once in a while: "Hey, I've been doing this job for. . . ." Well, Eileen: get a life! Learn to recruit, affirm, train and empower someone else. Then you can go on to other challenges and give up the doleful litany of "Always me . . . poor, poor me."

What does it take to gold star every family in your stack of cards?

I know how Henry Ford would answer that question. Mr. Ford had the highest regard for those who could empower others. When someone asked him what five qualities are needed for a leader to enable others to do, he replied "The number five quality is imagination; number four is imagination; number three is imagination; number two is imagination; and number one is— imagination."

All you need to empower others is imagination. Let's look at some everyday examples.

. . . *On the Subject of Teenagers*

The $64,000 question: How do you involve teens?

The Henry Ford answer: Imagination!

For its monthly food pantry collection, St. Mary Parish decided to distribute posters throughout the Township to encourage donations of food staples. Lynn, the Social Concerns Chairperson, called the local public high school and spoke to the art teacher.

"Keri, can you give me the names of some talented art students from our parish?"

Eleven names were offered, and Lynn made the calls.

"Hi. This is Lynn Roth from St. Mary's. Would Tim be home?"

"Sure, just a minute. I'll get him."

Tim pensively picks up the phone.

"Tim, this is Lynn from St. Mary's. I was talking to your art teacher and she said you've really got a gift with art. I want to ask you a favor. We're having our monthly food collection in three weeks, and I was hoping that you could design a poster advertising the event. If you can help, I'll drop off all the supplies at your house. We'd like to hang your poster in the church lobby."

"Yeah, I guess I can."

None of the eleven teens approached said "no." It's just a matter of asking the right teens to do the right jobs at the right times.

Three weeks later, the monthly food collection produced more donations than usual. Some of the posters decorating the church lobby and local stores boasted electric guitars motifs. Now I don't know what guitars have to do with food pantries, but they surely attract attention! The teen artists designed in their own unique styles . . . delivered the posters to church . . . brought friends in to see their handiwork.

Then they each received a thank you note: "Tim, your poster helped us go over the top on last week's food collection. Electric guitars must really turn people on!"

When you next need posters, it would be a big mistake not to call on Tim and his fellow artists.

Imagination! You as part of a leadership group, are charged with involving others. The right job + the right person = em-POWERment.

. . . *On the Subject of Bingo*

I co-chaired a weekly midnight bingo in my parish for nine years. As the substantial bingo revenues generated were used to subsidize our parish elementary school, I took my assignment very seriously. Parents of our school children were asked to volunteer to work either fifteen regular bingos during the course of a year or nine midnight (hardship) bingos.

Even with the enticement of six fewer nights per year of bingo work, it was still difficult to get a sufficient number of volunteers to come out at midnight . . . and those who did come let it be known that they were there under duress! What could be done to change their collective negative attitude? How could we "empower" them so that they would feel a sense of ownership for this project?

Together with my co-chairs, Katy and Martin, I scheduled a

meeting with the whole team. "We're short on volunteers, so we're asking you to consider a challenge. If any of you would be willing to volunteer for fifteen bingos per year instead of your required nine, we will teach you how to do everything: be paymaster, handle the financial duties, call the numbers . . . whatever you think you would like to do. We'll teach you. (Almost like loading a dishwasher!) And if you do agree to work fifteen bingos, we'll give you the gift of gifts." We then unveiled these navy blue shirts with the words "MIDNIGHT MARVELS" emblazoned in gold across the front. "Work fifteen bingos and you will become the proud owner. . . ." That shirt became the prestige symbol in St. Thomas the Apostle Parish. In no time our entire team was in uniform.

To empower someone is to say, "I'm taking you on; I'm going to train you, and then I'm going to let you run with it. You're such an important part of this endeavor that your absence is missed sorely. When you are here you make a real difference.

. . . *On the Subject of Cake Sales*

A very traditional fund-raiser for parish organizations is the Sunday morning cake sale. While meeting with one of our Rosary Society executive boards recently, I asked: "Who bakes those sinfully delicious goodies that you offer for sale twice a year?"

"Each member donates two homebaked items so that we can raise the funds we need to carry out our goals."

"How long does it take to bake two cakes?" (I really have to ask that question because to me baking involves buying a Pillsbury Chocolate Chip Cookie Mix Roll, cutting the slices into four equal parts and placing gently in the oven 'til they smell SUPER!

Whether it takes forty-five minutes or three hours to bake those two cakes, my advice is: "Don't do it!" At your Executive Board meeting, go to that stack of cards . . . pick out four or five unstarred cards with the names of people that you know, call each of your potential bakers and say: "Hi, Judy. At last night's Rosary meeting, we were talking about our upcoming cake sale and I got to thinking about your World Famous Green Apple Pie. . . ."

Certainly, you have to do your homework before you make your calls, but that's part of being a leader—knowing the special gifts of your people. Judy (and Ann, Frank, Alice and Marylou) bakes—not one, but two—pies (cakes, breads . . .) brings them to church and is involved. When she receives a warm thank you note from the Rosary Society president saying, "This was our most successful cake sale ever—thanks to you," she has earned a gold star on her family cards —and you have earned a gold star as an emPOWERer.

Why was it the most successful cake sale ever? Because you spent 45 minutes making phone calls instead of baking *two* cakes and, in the trade-off, you enlisted five "new" bakers who donated *ten* items for sale. Your job as a leader is to stop doing, to put your imagination into overtime, to empower!

. . . On the Subject of Car Raffles

The Holy Name Society of All Saints Parish sponsors an annual car raffle in conjunction with the parish's summer carnival—and the Holy Name members coordinate and manage all of the raffle components. While visiting one night with the executive board, I asked: "What happened to your resolution about involving new people in your projects?"

"Well, Eileen, we thought about sharing the work load, but it's an important fund-raiser, and we have it down to a science. . . ."

"Let's talk about it for ten minutes, and if, at the end of that time we haven't come up with a viable plan to include others, I'll rest my case. Fair enough?"

So for the next few minutes, we brainstormed. Suddenly, Bob, one of the trustees, said: "You know, I just thought of someone who could be a great help. Remember Catherine Snyder, the head teller at National Bank who was involved in that three-car accident last Christmas? She was seriously hurt, confined to a wheel-chair, a shut-in. But, boy, was she great with finances, figures and deposits. I wonder if she would be interested in working on the raffle."

The next morning Bob paid Catherine a visit.

"Catherine, The Holy Name will begin organizing its annual car raffle soon. We were hoping that you might consider helping us with the paperwork and bookkeeping."

"Well, I think I'd really like to be involved in helping the parish; but I'm locked into this apartment. How would the mailings get to the post office and the deposits to the bank?"

"We'll work that out."

Imagination! The Senior Citizens Club was approached to see if its members would be willing to pick up the mail in the morning (seniors seem to get up early), bring it over to Catherine's apartment and make the deposits at National Bank late each afternoon. The seniors agreed, and five teams each took responsibility for a different weekday.

Great. All of a sudden, Catherine had two visitors every morning and every afternoon. That first morning, she just accepted the mail and said, "Thank You." But on the second morning one of the seniors brought a few donuts, so Catherine put on a pot of coffee and they sat down to chat. By the third morning the coffee was brewing when her "new friends" arrived. Every morning and afternoon there were two visitors bringing news and companionship to Catherine—and each of her days was occupied with the meaningful task of "running the raffle." Records were kept meticulously, deposits were a work of art, additional raffle books were in the mail five minutes after being requested . . . and in Catherine's spare time, she "worked the phone"—calling all of her past customers, businesses and individuals alike, and charming them into promoting the raffle.

Catherine was so excited about once again contributing service to her parish—and so very gracious to all of the volunteers who were helping her to carry out her assignment. Her attitude wasn't one of "Here I am—stuck with the raffle again!" On the night of the drawing, Bob escorted Catherine into All Saints Parish Hall where she had the honor of drawing the name of the lucky winner of the car. When she pulled out that ticket, the applause that followed was more for Catherine than for anything else! She, along with the Seniors who had been her partners in the project, had been a vital part of one small piece of parish life. They had been emPOWERed—and everyone had gained through the experience.

What does it take? It takes imagination by leaders who have committed themselves to allowing others to feel ownership.

There is an ancient proverb which proclaims: "The greatest

leader is one who, when the job is done, can hear the people say, "We did it ourselves."

"D" is for Dismiss

Don't let anyone stay in the same position forever. It is difficult to remain enthusiastic, creative and committed to the same job year after year. Not only does a person run the risk of becoming set and stale in his/her approach, but that same person is being denied the opportunity to grow. Dismiss with joy, just as you recruited with joy. If you do not presently hold an annual night of appreciation for all the volunteers in your parish or school—whether it's a full course dinner, wine and cheese, or coffee and cake—institute it! Invite *everyone* who has done *something* during the year to attend, and say "Thank you" with great joy.

There are three important factors to remember about dismissing. First, if someone is leaving a leadership position, whether parish council, committee chairmanship, or organization executive board, take the time to formally evaluate the experience with that person. Also, if you were the one responsible for initially recruiting the volunteer, evaluate your effectiveness: did you successfully affirm, train and empower that person?

One of my childhood idols was football hero Johnny Unitas, quarterback of the then Baltimore Colts. His quote on evaluation: "For every hour of play we witness on a football field, there are *forty-nine* hours of evaluation that have gone before it."

Yet we seem to avoid evaluation. We're afraid of the word, which conjures up images of criticism, imperfections and failure. But evaluation should not be negative. It's a time for me to say, "Thank you for the service you gave. How did we do as a team? Do you think you're leaving your ministry a bit closer to God? A little more skilled in volunteer work? Did I do my job? How could we have done things differently?"

Evaluation is positive if it is two-way and if it is carried out in a climate of love and mutual respect. As a leader you have to acquire the skills to make sure that that is the way it is done.

The second factor is the "Thank you." This should be done in two phases: public and private. When people you have recruited leave their positions, send them a little gift—a pen, a box of candy, a plant, stationery—along with your note of thanks. The fact that people are acknowledged by the person who recruited them provides a very powerful incentive for them to re-volunteer in the future.

While the private "Thank you" is essential, the public gesture of thanks should not be overlooked. One special way to thank recruits, in addition to the night of appreciation, is through the parish bulletin. While the bulletin should never be used to recruit (remember, recruiting is done in person!), it is a very effective way of thanking people publicly. Thank volunteers who have completed their terms of service with a note about their particular accomplishments. Parishioners will appreciate reading about their friends and neighbors. That will probably be the most popular column in the bulletin.

Finally, when dismissing, send your volunteers forth with a good feeling about themselves and their contributions to the parish family. Invite them to investigate the full range of volunteer positions available for their future consideration. If their experience with you as recruiter and supporter has been positive, you will be confident in predicting that they will be back.

And now, you are dismissed. Go forth in love to serve the Lord!

Council Spirituality: Foundation for Mission

by Marie Kevin Tighe, SP

The key concept that undergirds the phrase "council spirituality" is that corporate spirituality is expressed quite differently from the spirituality of any one person. The life of a group is different from the life of any one of its members, and it is more than the sum of the lives of all of its members. The council which succeeds in developing itself as a true corporate entity will have a spirituality of its own. In such a council the members are willing to integrate their giftedness, their wisdom and their differences to serve a common mission. A council which achieves this kind of corporate identity is much more than just a collection of individuals. Parishioners may be elected or appointed to a structure called a council, but election or appointment involves only individual persons. Councils must be formed and developed. If the members do achieve corporate identity, the likelihood of the mission of the parish being well served is enhanced. The spirituality of the council will need to be developed, and from time to time, the council will need to evaluate and renew itself, as we shall see later in this chapter.

Spirituality in groups reveals itself in many ways. Following are a few of the key contributors to council spirituality:

- quality of personal presence
- genuine dialogue
- life-giving and effective group climate
- prayer, reflection and a capacity for discernment toward shared decision-making

Such a spirituality calls for a commitment of member to member and a true sense of mutuality around a common purpose or mission. So then, let us suppose that we are in the process of forming and developing a council. Just what is "council spirituality" and how does it come about? Council spirituality is a mysterious bonding in faith, hope and love, which takes place within a group of persons who share a common vision toward which God is calling them. In councils, it is the other side of the coin of personal spirituality; it does not replace personal spirituality. The way in which a group comes to a shared vision has its beginning in developing a high quality of personal presence to one another, and then expanding that into dialogic presence by developing a capacity for genuine dialogue. These characteristics will allow the council to gather, to distill, and to integrate the wisdom of the group. If each one possesses some truth, then the truth will be more adequately expressed in all of us than in any one of us taken singly. Determining together just how we shall pursue the mission entrusted to us requires prayer, discernment and the management of a great deal of information. We must listen to the Spirit within ourselves and try to discern the movement of that same Spirit in other council members. We need to ask often, "What do we hear ourselves saying?" That is, how does the Spirit seem to be speaking through us as a body? It is important, too, to listen to the wider parish, to the civic community, and to the many voices and events calling to us from the larger world.

The council is called to be a community for the sake of the larger community of the parish, just as the church is for the sake of the world. We are based in community and in organization so that we can be for the world a more effective herald, sacrament, and servant. The council does not exist just to make things nicer for us here in the parish. Councils, as well as individuals, must be attentive to, adhere to, and be abandoned to, the creative, sustaining, redeeming, commissioning love of God. Approaching council work in this way may require that we let go of many of our pet ideas and personal agendas. It shifts us away from the power of domination toward a sensitivity to the power of the Holy Spirit moving within the council. Such an enablement of power is a sign of God's mystical presence in the church.

Let us look intently now at each of the four characteristics that were mentioned earlier as revelatory of council spirituality.

Quality of Personal Presence

Personal presence is far more than bodily presence. It requires us to be "all there" for the other person or persons with whom we are in relationship or with whom we are called to relationship. The quality of presence is measured by the degree to which persons are involved with each other as they communicate. We may speak of five levels of presence, each level being prerequisite for the next with the fifth level being the highest.

Level One: Attentiveness is rudimentary to the development of a high level of presence. That to which one is attentive controls in great measure what is allowed into awareness. Attentiveness requires eye contact and listening, but not yet responding. In the wonderful little book, *Real Presence,* by Regis Duffy, OFM, we are reminded: "Presence is, of course, more than attention. It is self-gift and enabling love."[1] Attentiveness is the first step toward the lofty goals of "self-gift and enabling love."

Examples of attentiveness in the life of Jesus:

Matthew 14: 14–21	Feeding of the five thousand
Matthew 19: 27–30	Hundred-fold reward
Luke 7:43–48	Woman with hemorrhage
John 13: 1–29	Washing of feet

Level Two: Understanding. In an effort to understand another we move beyond the listening required for attentiveness to a more active listening, which attempts to grasp ideas and context as well as the lived reality of the person of the speaker. Risk and vulnerability cut across all levels of vulnerability associated with one's willingness to understand others and to be understood by others. Father Charles Curran, the psychologist who taught for many years at Loyola University in Chicago, once said, "If we ever really fully understood another person, that person would be totally acceptable to us." It is a level of presence worth striving to achieve.

Examples of understanding in the life of Jesus:

Matthew 9:36	"The sight of the people moved him to pity"
Luke 10:38–42	Martha and Mary
Luke 19:41–44	Weeping over Jerusalem

Level Three: Responding. The third level of presence, is a kind of mid-point in the growth of a person trying to develop a high quality of presence. It is at this juncture that one becomes more involved, listening not only to the speaker, but also listening to one's **own reactions** to the content of what is being said. Responding reveals both power and influence. By responding to the experience, insights or situations of others, we allow them to exert influence and power over us. Reciprocally, we are allowed to exert influence and power over them. This is not undue influence, nor is it the power of domination. Rather, genuine mutual response has great potential for both individual and group growth. It is the power of enablement and the influence for good.

Examples of responding in the life of Jesus:

Mark 10:17–27	Rich young man
John 9:1–41	Cure of the blind man
Luke 24:13–32	Emmaus

Level Four: Committed Responding allows us to explore differences with respect by remaining in creative tension with those holding different viewpoints. At the fourth level we arrive at the threshold of a very high quality of personal presence. Committed response reveals caring. There is a willingness to respond when there is no guarantee of agreement. Perhaps there may even be a threat of losing something of what one has or would prefer. This fourth level is an indication of a real and a very high quality of caring in relationships.

Examples of committed responding in the life of Jesus:

Luke 22:47–48	Betrayal of Jesus
Mark 9:30–37	"Unless you become as little children . . ."
Luke 23:32–34	"Father, forgive them . . ."

Level Five: Calling. One must have progressed steadily and whole-heartedly through the first four levels before reaching the final level of calling. This stage is often referred to as affirming, promoting, or challenging to greater growth. Having reached the stage of genuine caring in level four, one always desires that the other achieve the fullness of his or her potential. Only those who have "radiated worth to other" as Raul Plus, SJ, reminds us, may take the liberty of calling or challenging others to greater integrity. When the members of a council have reached this quality of presence, they are then free to call each other both personally and as a group to greater authenticity and integrity. This is a peak moment in the spiritual life of the council.

Examples of calling in the life of Jesus:

Matthew 12:46–50	"Who are my mother and sister and brother?"
Mark 4:37–41	Storm at sea
John 4:8–42	Woman at the well

These five levels are, of course, meant to be integrated rather than thought of in isolation from one another. To work at developing a high quality of personal presence is essential to growth in the spiritual life.

Genuine Dialogue

Dialogue is a synthesis of divergent views under a unifying concept. According to Howe, "Dialogue is that address and response between persons in which there is a flow of meaning between them in spite of all the obstacles which normally would block the relationship."[2] Dialogue does not mean shooting darts of privatized wisdom at one another in some kind of orderly manner. Some of us may have to learn new ways of interacting that are more compatible with our identity as church, ways different from those to which we may be accustomed in other arenas. When we hear the expression "dialogue toward mutuality," we understand it to mean a process of consensual decision making which is the normal outcome of genuine dialogue.

Many of us come from other than council situations in which we sit around a table to discuss and to plan for some aspect of our daily work or for some civic project. Some of what we do there is transferable; some of it is not. The church is an organization simply by virtue of numbers and the need for good order, but the Church is much more than that. We are a community of faith, a mystical expression of the extended life of Jesus in the here and now. We may need to help one another in learning and using words and practices such as: discernment, dialogue and consensus, all of which have a special meaning in the Christian community setting. The kind of decision-making we employ may be quite different from the usual win-lose strategy of voting. Any council of good will can learn the art of fruitful dialogue, consensus-seeking and consensual decision making. A friend used to speak of this as "arriving at the uncoerced persuasion" of the community. Of course, consensus does not mean that we are all in total agreement, but it does mean that everyone has participated in the dialogue and that everyone has been listened to with respect. Such an approach requires that the decision be reached by using predetermined criteria acceptable to the council as well as a value-base that is consistent with the identity of the council as a church group. The following account has much to say to pastoral councils:

> Recently a group of ministers was told that until the Church becomes a community it will not be able to communicate adequately. Left unanswered was the question: How does the Church or any group of people become a community? And the answer is simple: it becomes a community when as persons, the members enter into dialogue with one another and assume responsibility for the common life. Without this dialogue, individuals and society are abstractions. It is through dialogue that we accomplish the miracle of personhood and community.[3]

The purpose of dialogue is mutual learning and mutual growth. Dialogic presence is one step up from personal presence. It allows us to engage one another in things that really matter. Such a degree of personal and dialogic presence will bring an element of true peace—

always a sign of the Holy Spirit—to any group, and will encourage a greater willingness to stay in whatever inevitable struggles emerge in the ongoing life of the group. It seems appropriate to close this section on dialogue with one last reference to the classical work, *The Miracle of Dialogue:*

> Dialogue is to love what blood is to the body. When the flow of blood stops, the body dies. When dialogue stops, love dies and resentment and hate are born. But dialogue can restore a dead relationship. Indeed, this is the miracle of dialogue; it can bring relationship into being, and it can bring into being once again a relationship that has died.[4]

The spirituality of a council is apparent to members and observers alike, as they experience the movement toward the articulation of a shared vision for the parish faith community. The process is one of integrative change, a true inner conversion of heart.

Climate—Life-giving and Effective

The third indication of council spirituality comes from the generally pervasive climate which exists in the group. Climate in group is a function of two factors: 1) the quality of relationships which exist between and among the members, and 2) the clarity each member, as well as the council as a whole, has about the overall purpose/mission of the council. The following diagram helps to understand these two dimensions of group climate:

C	(Supportive)		(Purposive)
O			Corporate people of mission
M			
M			
U		(Practical)	
N			
I			
T			
Y	(Routine)		(Task-directed)

(Left axis reads: COMMUNITY)

MISSION[5]

Most councils move around on this grid from time to time. However, having a conceptual framework like this for the purpose of evaluation can often be helpful. It is not only a tool of assessment, but an instrument which could provide inspiration for growth in council spirituality. The upper right-hand corner is the ultimate goal. Growth in a true spirit of community and growth in commitment to the mission can move the council in this direction. Following are some lists of characteristics of councils which might be "diagnosed" as being either at the lower end or the higher end of the scales of COMMUNITY and MISSION:

Community (Quality of relationships)

Lower end of scale	*Upper end of scale*
—impersonal	—committed to each other's growth
—superficial	—challenging/accepting challenges
—non-supportive	—genuinely concerned for one another
—non-committed	—differences valued
—denigrating	—mutual respect
—secretive	—open dialogue
—competitive	—teamwork
—distant	—caring
—indifferent	—solicitous

Mission (Clarity of purpose and commitment)

Lower end of scale	*Upper end of scale*
—aimless	—focused
—random activity	—clarity of purpose
—disorganized	—organized
—activity directed	—goal directed
—duplication of effort	—shared responsibility
—independent	—interdependent
—dispersed	—regular evaluation
—minimal evaluation	—integration of learning/ evaluation

One can easily see an example of a deep corporate spirituality in the council which generally hovers on the upper end of the scale. Persons of modest capabilities who are able, as a group, to achieve an effective and life-giving group climate will, in all likelihood, be more productive over the long range than highly talented individuals working in a poor group climate. This knowledge and the application of its principles, is the "stuff" of council spirituality. The way we are with one another and our commitment to sacred mission entrusted to us, will be the everyday expression of our deepest spiritual values. The Second Vatican Council teaches that "The function of the Church is to render God present and, as it were, visible in the world."[6] On the following diagram we see the two points of the star, "Community" and "Organization" supporting the other three points of "Herald," "Sacrament" and "Servant." Such a model keeps before us the ways in which we are to "render God present and . . . visible." This solemn responsibility can be realized only by parishes and councils which have a strong foundation in the spiritual life. For how can we be authentic as Herald, Sacrament and Servant unless we are in communion with one another and desire ardently to serve the mission entrusted to us by Jesus?

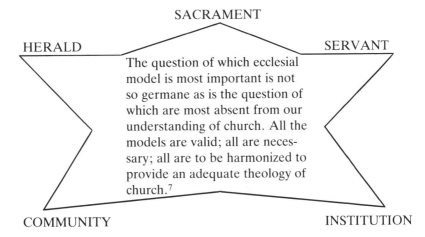

SACRAMENT

HERALD

SERVANT

The question of which ecclesial model is most important is not so germane as is the question of which are most absent from our understanding of church. All the models are valid; all are necessary; all are to be harmonized to provide an adequate theology of church.[7]

COMMUNITY

INSTITUTION

Prayer, Reflection, Discernment

The life of the council needs to be "shot through" with prayer, reflection and discernment. These are mentioned last because they permeate all of the other characteristics of council spirituality mentioned here. The work of the council is carried out best in an atmosphere and in an awareness of God's presence. "Book-end prayer" performed perfunctorily at the beginning and the end of meetings is not adequate. While we may begin with a reading and prayerful reflection on scripture, it is very appropriate from time to time in the course of the meeting, to pause briefly and to examine quietly, the way in which the Spirit of God seems to be moving the group. Maintaining such an atmosphere is conducive to insuring that we treat the work of the council as a sacred trust. Although efficiency and expediency are laudable qualities for any council to pursue, it is important that prayer, reflection and discernment are never sacrificed in their name. In addition to formal periods of prayer, time needs to be given to allow for serious reflection on issues moving toward decision. This reflection is not just mulling over things in light of one's personal insights alone. A council must weigh its issues in light of the gospel principles and values, the call of the church, the signs of the times, and in consideration of the wisdom, concerns and needs of the parish at large. Prayer, information gathering, discussion and reflection prepare a council for the final stages of discernment toward decision.

In examining the pros and cons of a certain issue, we are guided by far weightier criteria than personal likes or dislikes. Holding criteria for decision making to values and principles that are deeper than personal preference will bring about more peaceful resolutions to even difficult concerns.

In order to nourish the spiritual life of the council it seems essential that at least twice a year, a day or an evening and a day be spent in a kind of retreat workshop. At times such as these, the agenda is put aside and the council gives itself to a period of extended prayer and reflection. This provides an opportunity to examine in depth, the four characteristics of council spirituality which have been described here:

1) Quality of personal presence
2) Genuine dialogue
3) Climate: life-giving and effective
4) Prayer, reflection and discernment

Before persons are elected or otherwise chosen to be a member of the council, it should be understood that participation in days of formation and development, as well as days of retreat, are all a part of the obligation one is assuming. The days of retreat are opportunities for both personal and corporate renewal. These are graced times, when each member can examine his or her quality of participation and contribution and, if necessary, make a renewed commitment. It is, as well, a time for corporate renewal for the council as a whole when the group can examine its integrity and authenticity as a leadership group. Councils as corporate persons may also want to recommit themselves at such a time. It would be important for the whole parish to know that the council has had such an experience. Better still, the parish would have been asked to pray for the success of such a renewal event. The life cycle of a council includes, then, formation, development and renewal in ever-recurring rhythms. Councils that are aware of and responsive to these rhythms are powerful instruments for good in the parish community and beyond.

Conclusion

The Second Vatican Council addressed the responsibility of all the baptized for developing the communion of persons which is the church, and for promoting the mission entrusted to us by Jesus. The council also developed and taught an ecclesiology which emphasized the church as the people of God.

To be "a people" is to have a common heritage, to share a common life, and to move together on a common journey. This journey is the journey of life, the journey of faith. From time to time we come together to pray, to discern and to choose the best ways, in this time and place, to exercise our mission and to authenticate our Christian presence to the world. This is the particular work of the pastoral council in collaboration with the pastor. Many of us may remember a time when we thought that these responsibilities belonged to only a few people in the church. The teachings of Vatican Council II remind us again and again that all of us together are God's people, the church, and that all of us are responsible in some way for the life and mission of the church. That, indeed, calls us to be the church in a new way. If all of us are responsible, then all of us need channels through which we can exercise this responsibility. The pastoral council is one such channel. It is a means of a church community's envisioning a future which will further the reign of God. It will require a well-formed, well-developed council with a solid corporate spirituality. Careful pastoral planning with broad participation must be done in order to articulate a mission which embodies the vision. Then it will be necessary to chart the course of events, the programs of action, the allocation of resources of personnel, time, energy, facilities and finances, in such a way as to move effectively toward the realization of the mission. Councils which are rooted and grounded in a spirituality of the group will have a strong foundation for mission.

Notes

[1]Duffy, Regis, OFM, *Real Presence: Worship, Sacraments and Commitment,* Harper and Row (San Francisco, 1982), p. 3.

[2]Howe, Reuel L., *The Miracle of Dialogue,* The Seabury Press (New York, 1963), p. 37.

[3]Howe, *Ibid.,* p. 5

[4]Howe, *Ibid.,* p. 3

[5]Based on Blake-Mouton Managerial Grid.

[6]Flannery, Austin, OP, Ed., *Vatican Council II: The Conciliar and Post-Conciliar Documents,* The Liturgical Press (Collegeville, MN 1975), p. 721.

[7]Adapted from *The Parish as Learning Community,* by Thomas Downs, Paulist Press, 1979.

The Parish Pastoral Council and Prayer

by Kathleen Turley, RSM

The Second Vatican Council emphasized that each baptized person is called to holiness, to fulfill the mission of Jesus in our world. Christians are called to read the signs of our times and to respond to needs in the manner Jesus would if he were on earth today. As members of parish pastoral councils, you are leaders who must set the stage and espouse a vision of what the future of the church can be. Your task as leaders is to take your people from where they are now to where they have not been. You present a vision of what parish can be and facilitate people to move toward that vision. Implementation of a vision does not take place instantly; that vision must be articulated and repeated over and over again in a variety of ways.

The purpose of this chapter is to underscore your role in forming a community of faith which is nourished by prayer and to illustrate how serving on a parish pastoral council can be a faith heightening experience.

Faith Nourished by Prayer

As parish pastoral council members you form a community of faith that comes together in love and prayer to try to discern what the Holy Spirit is saying to you in this parish, at this moment, in this time in history. Faith enables you to look beyond and see something more. There is an old story of three people who viewed a sunrise over the ocean. The first person looked at the red ball on the horizon and said, "It is going to rain all day." The second person recognized the beauty of nature and appreciated the gorgeous view. The third person exclaimed, "Praise God!" The third viewer saw the sunrise with the eyes of faith and recognized in it the presence of God. Parish pastoral council members have an opportunity to become faith-filled leaders who take people where they are and bring them to where they have not been.

As believers, our faith allows us to move beyond the challenges and the burdens to see the blessings. Faith enables us to see God's presence in those around us: our neighbor, our friend, our children, our fellow pastoral council members, the homeless old woman pushing the grocery cart filled with all her possessions, the drug addict, the alcoholic begging on the street corner, the teenage boy with AIDS, and on and on. Faith empowers us to reach out to the needy and to minister to and with them. Faith is nourished by prayer, both personal and communal. In his book, *The Ways of Prayer: An Introduction,* Michael Pennock writes, "Each of us is a word of God, speaking God's love and goodness to the rest of the world."

Someone once asked me, "How well do you think you pray?" I responded, "Observe how I live and you can tell me how well I pray." The fruits of our prayer are revealed in the acts of living. Prayer is the ongoing relationship with God out of which our personal ministry flows. Therefore, it is essential that we make time for personal prayer even if it's only five minutes a day.

There are many ways to pray: read and reflect on a chapter or passage from the Old or New Testament or the daily scripture readings. Some people prefer saying the rosary or carrying on a personal conversation with God. Others engage in some type of meditation for 15–20 minutes each day. Studies have shown that meditation is a way of reducing stress. Problems are not solved, but attitudes toward the problems change. A relationship with God is developed very much the way a personal friendship is developed. One finds as many ways as possible to spend time with and get to know the friend better.

It is important for some to have a prayer place. For me often my car is my prayer place because I spend so much time in it. For one mother of three, her prayer place is the bathroom, the one place where she can have privacy. Others prefer the kitchen where they can pray while preparing meals. It is not the place where we pray or how we pray that is important, but **that we pray,** for unless we have some time for God and God alone, we will not be transformed.

Prayer and the Council Meeting

A few years ago our bishop gave a keynote address at the Annual Diocesan Parish Pastoral Council Convening, in which he traced the history of parish pastoral councils in our diocese, described their role today and the qualities parish pastoral council members should cultivate. One of those qualities is that parish pastoral council members should be men and women of prayer who at their council meetings should allow quality time for prayer, about a half hour. The prayer the bishop was advocating was not bookend prayer, that which opens and closes a meeting, but prayer that moves hearts and changes lives.

It is important that a substantial amount of time be devoted to prayer at the parish pastoral council meeting. There are many resources available to assist in the preparation of prayer. A list of resources is included at the end of this chapter. Introducing council members to a variety of prayer forms can be a learning and yet a fresh experience.

A Telling Example

There was one parish pastoral council which had for three years stated that meaningful prayer at meetings would be a priority for that year. At the beginning of the fourth year the council president stated, "Each year we say that prayer at meetings is a priority and each year we do very little to make it a reality. This year I propose we set aside fifteen minutes at every meeting for prayer. Since there are twelve members on our council, each member will be responsible for coordinating prayer for one month. Select a person from scripture, either Old or New Testament. When the agenda is sent out two weeks prior to the meeting, it will include the scripture passages on which to pray and reflect for the upcoming meeting."

Most of the members felt that the idea was excellent. Mike,

the chair of the buildings and grounds committee, disagreed. Mike was the person who set up for all the meetings and then cleaned up when everyone went home. Mike thought adding this to the agenda would just make each meeting longer and make his arrival home that much later. Since everyone else thought the idea was good, the president assured Mike that it would not lengthen the meeting too much. Also everyone could help close up. The proposal was accepted and the year began.

When it was Mike's turn to coordinate the prayer, the council president approached him and said, "I know you did not want to pray this way. If you would like, I would be happy to take your turn." To which Mike responded, "No, each month I have prayed all these passages and I have been waiting my turn." Mike's selection of a scriptural person was Martha, and his opening remarks went something like this: "All my life I've been a 'Martha'. My dad died when I was in high school and I became 'Dad' to my younger brothers and sisters. When my mother became ill, I took care of her until she died. All of you know my wife is an invalid and needs constant care. I know I was against this idea initially, but praying the scripture passages has given me the opportunity to be Mary."

Then the pastor stood up, opened a folded sheet and began to read:

Dear members of the Parish Pastoral Council:

During these past few months Mike has been a different person. Usually serious and intense, he now walks around the house singing. He has taken time to read poetry, to listen to music, to bring me flowers, to enjoy life. The twinkle in his eye and zip in his stride has returned. Thank you for giving me back the kind and sensitive man I married.

Sincerely, Mrs. Mike

Other Methods

This is the prayer that changes lives. Using people from scripture is just one way of praying. Reflection and dialogue on the daily scriptural readings or a particular theme are other variations of this style. Other approaches may be the recitation of the rosary on occasion. Currently there is a resurgence of devotion to and interest in Mary, the Mother of God. Other ideas are: evening prayer from the liturgy of the hours, creative prayer services, guided meditation and an annual day of retreat where the council can spend an extended time in prayer. Not only does this provide members an opportunity to deepen their prayer life, but it also is a time for community building.

One rural parish meets each month for a pot luck supper and scripture reflection before the council meeting. This enables members to get to know one another and interact on a social as well as a business level to build community and trust. Creating a level of trust among the group is critical in decision making, especially when those decisions impact on a total parish community.

What is the role of prayer in decision making on a council? The challenge for members is to discern what the Spirit is saying to this group of people. It is not enough to pray at the beginning of the meeting and then make decisions with no further consideration of this. A pastor told me of an experience he had with his pastoral council where the group was engaged in a heated debate that was going nowhere. After about forty minutes, the youth representative on the council suggested that the group could break for ten minutes to reflect on the conversation and consider what Jesus would do in this situation. When the group gathered again, they came to consensus very quickly. There are some groups who routinely, after an issue has been thoroughly discussed, take a five minute prayer/reflection break, then reassemble to make a decision.

Council members must ask themselves how the decision they are about to enact will enhance the mission of Jesus. Since the mission of the parish is to proclaim gospel values, every decision should be reviewed through the lens of those values.

After the council meeting, possibly enroute home if you travel alone, it is helpful to do a self-evaluation of the meeting using questions such as these: What happened at the meeting that promoted gospel values? Did I truly represent to the best of my ability the best interests of the parish? Were my actions at this meeting consistent with my personal call to holiness?

The call to holiness is an invitation to make visible for the whole world the meaning of a just society. The attainment of a just society is facilitated by faith-filled leaders who are rooted in the message and mission of Jesus.

Selected Resources

THE BIBLE

Conroy, Maureen   *Journey of Love: God Moving in our Hearts and Lives,* Paulist Press, 1993

Dalrymple, John   *Simple Prayer,* Michael Glazier, 1984

DeMello, Anthony   *Wellsprings*
                               Song of the Bird
                               One Minute Wisdom

Hays, Edward   *Prayers for the Domestic Church: A Handbook for Worship in the Home*

                               Pray All Ways
                               Reflections on a modern mysticism . . . where the ordinary contains the extraordinary in a daily communion with the divine mystery

                               Prayers for a Planetary Pilgrim
                               A personal manual for prayer and ritual
                               A Pilgrim's Almanac, Forest of Peace Books, Inc., Easton, Kansas

Hintz, Debra

Gathering Prayers: Prayer Services for Parish Meetings, Twenty Third Publication, Mystic, Ct.
Each book has a collection of complete prayer services

Pennock, Michael F.

The Ways of Prayer: An Introduction, Ave Maria Press, 1987

Rossetti, Stephen

I Am Awake: Discovering Prayer, Paulist Press, 1987

Schaffran, Janet and Pat Kozak

More than Words: Prayer and Ritual for Inclusive Communities, Meyer-Stone Books, 1988

Parish Pastoral Councils: Responding to Cultural Diversity

by Nancy A. Pineda, M.Div.

Introduction

One of the greatest gifts within the U.S. church today is its cultural diversity. And yet it remains one of the church's greatest challenges. While the reality of cultural diversity has been present in the church since its beginnings, perhaps at no other time in our recent history has this topic been as widely discussed by U.S. Catholic Church leadership and faithful alike. Pastoral council members, as leaders within parish communities, need to grapple with the complex realities and significance of the culturally diverse faith communities which they serve.[1]

Why is cultural diversity such an important question for us today? Why are we so focused on and concerned about cultural inclusivity? From where does the passion for these questions stem? Many factors have contributed to the heightened importance of our awareness and understanding of diversity.

As Americans, the civil rights movement in the 1960s pushed many of us, from those who lived at the margins to those who lived at the center, to begin a conscious reflection on the experience of race and culture in our society. For some, the reflection focused not only on personal experience but also on institutions and systems. Those thoughtful enough to understand the institutional and systemic dimensions asked questions like, "Why aren't Blacks proportionally represented in positions of leadership in all of society's institutions? Why are the high school graduation rates for Latinos, Native Americans and Pacific Islanders so abysmally low? As a result of this new consciousness, "separate but equal" was no longer the prevailing philosophy of most Americans. "Integration" became the rallying cry of the time. As Americans, we were deeply moved by the lives and stunned by the violent deaths of Dr. Martin Luther King, President John Kennedy, and his brother, presidential hopeful Robert Kennedy. Each in his own way captured the imagination of U.S. citizens and many others around the globe. These leaders challenged us as a nation to dream of something more, to dream of a promised land which embraced people of color more fully than it ever had before.

With the presidency of John F. Kennedy, the first and only Catholic president, U.S. Catholics came of age. After decades of religious hostility, a Catholic was finally trusted enough to be elected to the highest office of the land, signaling that the United States accepted American Catholics more fully than it ever had before.

In the 1960s, the church was likewise undergoing immense change. Not only were U.S. Catholics being challenged by the cry for racial equality which swept the country, we were also in the midst of a monumental evolution in our own ecclesial self-understanding. The Second Vatican Council brought this transformation into focus and sharpened it. For the first time in the history of episcopal councils, a truly global gathering took place. African bishops represented African Catholics. Latin American bishops and Asian bishops did the same for the Catholics of their countries. Never had the Catholic faithful of the world been represented by bishops who were one of their own. Karl Rahner, SJ, described Vatican II as "the Church's first official self-actualization as a world Church."[2] Bishops from Latin America, Asia and Africa found themselves bridging their Roman experience of the church with their experience of the church's unique inculturation in their own nations, among their own people.

While questions of race and culture came sharply to the fore in the 1960s, they have continued to mark our lives in the 1980s and 1990s. Recent years have seen the Los Angeles race riots, the beatings of Rodney King and Reginald Denny, the Anita Hill/ Clarence Thomas hearings, the Latino and African-American community uprisings in Miami, the California legislature's successful attempt to pass "English Only" laws, the native American fishing rights controversies in the Pacific Northwest and Upper Midwest, the ongoing scandalous and inhuman treatment of Mexican and Central American nationals by the U.S. Border Patrol, the strong emergence of white supremacy groups such as the skinheads and neo-Nazis, to name only a few. We are surrounded and constantly faced with what it means to live within a diverse society.

We face these same questions in our parish communities as well. We need to ask ourselves: is there room in our churches? Is there room for Filipinos, room for their celebrations of Flores de Mayo and the feast of San Lorenzo? Is there room for Korean prayers and hymns? Is there room for an image of Our Lady of Guadelupe? Is there room for mass in Spanish on Sunday morning rather than in the afternoon when no one else is using the church? Is there room for a statue of the Black Christ or of San Martin de Porres? Is there room for gospel choirs? Is there room for the sounds of Native American drums? Is there room for people of color around the pastoral council's table? Is there room in our hearts to hear Jesus' mandate to ". . . go, therefore, and make disciples of all nations"? (Matt 28:19) Well, is there room? How will pastoral council leadership respond?

In this chapter, I will explore the central question of culture as it relates to the work of pastoral councils in parishes, consider five parish models of cultural integration and the implications for pastoral councils, review some of the challenges pastoral councils face, and finally, discuss some of the important characteristics of a culturally inclusive parish.

The Question of Culture

Within our own parish communities, each of us will instinctively express our humanity in a particular manner which is characteristic of our ethnic group. We are almost always unaware that this is what we are doing. As human beings we are all enculturated. Enculturation may be described as

> . . . the process by which the human individual becomes inserted into his/her own culture. Unlike other animals,

human beings from the very moment of birth and through
a relatively long time are helpless creatures constantly in
need of support and training by others for almost all aspects of life. This "learning experience, which marks hu-
mans off from other creatures and by means of which,
initially and in later life, they achieve competence in their
culture, may be called enculturation."[3]

Even parishioners who are aware of this phenomenon, may not be
aware of the significance of its impact on the life of the parish
community. A parish which is culturally diverse, and few parishes
within the U.S. are not, finds itself in the midst of a cultural crisis,
in the middle of many different interpretations of what it means to
be human, and therefore, of what it means to be Catholic. These
different expressions of humanity and faith commingle in parish
communities, often much like water and oil, either not mixing at
all or doing so only briefly and tentatively. Most of the time we
don't realize or understand why it is so difficult to work effectively
and sensitively with culturally diverse faith communities, why the
gift and challenge of cultural diversity so eludes and baffles us.

The fundamental question is that of **culture** in its most profound sense. The term **culture** is popularly understood as the cloth-
ing we wear, the foods we eat, how we spend our free time, in
other words particular social behaviors and distinctive customs.
While these realities are certainly expressions of **culture, culture** is
much more profound. **Culture** is a way of life of a people; it fundamentally shapes our thought patterns, our emotional responses,
our values, our language, even the way we understand who we are
and how we are related to every dimension of our world. Our
culture pervades every aspect of our lives. This includes how we
relate to other human beings, to the institutions within our society,
to nature, to the divine and so forth. The following definition of
culture highlights an important distinction in our understanding of
the term.

. . . in the use of the term culture [there is a] distinction
between the two levels: the practical and the symbolical.
The practical aspect of culture bears on tangible realities:

the activities and ways of conduct of social life, tools and techniques, customs, forms of apprenticeship and instruction, etc. In one word: the social practice. The symbolic aspect indicates all that transmits meanings (be they conscious or unconscious) and representations between the members or the generations of a society: rites, traditions, myths, language, etc."[4]

It is the second level, the symbolic level of culture which is at the heart of our struggles to genuinely embrace cultural diversity in our parish communities. While we all passionately claim the Catholic faith as our own, we often interpret the symbols, rites and traditions of our Catholic faith differently. The meaning that these symbols, rites and traditions hold for distinct ethnic communities is beyond the power of words to express. It taps the very core of who we are. The image of Blessed Kateri Tekakwitha, a Catholic Mohawk Indian, does not evoke the same fervor of response from all Catholic faithful; neither do certain Christmas customs nor do celebrations in honor of the Vietnamese martyrs. Not all of us light votive candles and have conversations with saints, but some of us do, and for those who do, the devotional ritual is sacred. Some of us resonate deeply with a symbol of Jesus crucified, while others prefer an image of the resurrected Christ in their sanctuary. Images of Mary and rituals in her honor evoke a wide range of responses from Catholics. For some, Mary's image evokes a call to personal, pietistic devotion; for others, her image is prophetic and demands justice for the marginated, and for still others she does neither. As we live our faith, particular symbols, rites and traditions shape us. They shape our understanding of who we are and who we are before God. They form our world of meaning.

Our parish communities are one arena in which distinct worlds of meaning collide with one another. To bring together different ethnic groups and develop among them a shared experience of church which both respects the particularity of each and yet holds up the unity of us all is a formidable challenge. Most of us take our understanding of what it means to be human, our culture, for granted. It's an inherited "common sense." It is as innate to us as breathing. For any of us to respect another cultural group's understanding of its own humanity and recognize it is as valid as our own demands a radical openness on our part. Radical because we can never fully understand or appreciate a culture which is different from our own. Pastoral council members need to be aware of the significance of culture and the need for openness. This begins with a reflection on our own experience of culture. Below I have included some questions for this purpose:

Reflection Questions

1) Describe the neighborhood you grew up in.

— Ethnically
— Economically
— Religiously
— Linguistically

2) Where do you think you received the greatest influence in developing your attitudes toward various ethnic groups (African-Americans, Asian/Pacific Islanders, Latinos, Native-Americans, Western & Eastern European Americans)?

— Family
— School
— Media
— Neighborhood
— Parish

3) How has this influenced your interactions with these groups?

4) Describe the neighborhood you live in today.

— Ethnically
— Economically
— Religiously
— Linguistically

The pastor and the parish pastoral council are pivotal in the church's ability to respond effectively to the cultural diversity of their parish community. If a pastoral council is to authentically serve its parish community, its membership must reflect the diversity of the parish community. If a pastoral council does not reflect the ethnic diversity of its parish, it will, at best, lose credibility with many of its parishioners and, at worse, become a symbol of exclusion, a source of anger. For people of color the parish community can be one of the few places of acceptance in our society, a place in which to breathe freely and pray fully. Or, the parish community can be a very painful place in which a sense of self, of culture and of the sacred are not understood, much less cherished and nurtured.

At a deeper level, the question which pastors and pastoral council members must ask themselves is: "What is the church's role in the face of cultural integration?" "Will the church see its role primarily as an Americanizer, or an evangelizer, of cultures?" "Will it continue to insist—as it once did in the not too distant past—that to be Catholic one first had to be a 'good American'?"[5]

Pope Paul VI's exhortation entitled On Evangelization in the Modern World (1975)[6] sheds light on these questions. The following text represents one of the clearest discussions of the mission of the church within a culturally pluralistic world:

> . . . what matters is to evangelize human culture and cultures, not in a purely decorative way, as it were by applying a thin veneer, but in a vital way, in depth and right to their very roots . . .

> The Gospel, and therefore evangelization as well, cannot be identified with any particular culture but it is independent of all cultures. On the other hand, the reign of God which the Gospel proclaims takes concrete form in the lives of men [sic] who are profoundly shaped by their particular culture. It is also a fact that elements of man's [sic] culture and cultures must be used in building the Kingdom of God. Therefore, although the Gospel and evangelization do not properly belong to any culture, neither are they incompatible with any. On the contrary they

can enter into all of them without being subservient to any.

The split between the Gospel and culture is without a doubt the drama of our time, just as it was of other times. Therefore every effort must be made to ensure the full evangelization of culture, or more correctly cultures.[7]

In addition, the New Testament records many examples, taken from the life of Jesus and the experience of the early church, which illustrate the role of culture in relationship to faith. The following includes some of the more significant examples: the Samaritan woman (John 4:4–42); the Syro-Phoenician woman (Matt 15:21–28; Mark 7:24–30); the good Samaritan (Luke 10:29–37), Jesus, a "Galilean" Jesus (John 7:40–52); Pentecost (Acts 2:4–12); Peter's vision and the call of the gentiles (Acts 10:9–11:26). Pastors and pastoral council members need to reflect on the gospel and the tradition as they consider different ways in which they might respond to cultural diversity.

Reflection: Scripture

1) Read through one of the above scripture passages. Spend some time with the passage in silent prayer.

2) Use your imagination as you consider the scripture passage. Do you identify with any of the individuals mentioned in the passage? If so, how do you think this individual felt? Why did she or he act as they did? As you read through the passage, do any images come to mind?

3) Allow the scripture passage to illuminate your ministry as a pastoral council member. What new insights come to mind? What does the passage have to offer the pastoral council as it considers cultural diversity?

Reflection: Magisterium

1) Read through and prayerfully consider the above selection from the writings of Pope Paul VI. Which ideas do you find stimulating?

2) Find a copy of Evangelii Nutiandi, On Evangelization in the Modern World. Read the text and schedule time during a pastoral council meeting to discuss it.[8]

After considering the significance of culture and reflecting on the vision and values we hold as Catholics, the pastoral and pastoral council's task becomes much more focused. How are we called to respond to cultural diversity within our parish? How do we structure our parish community in such a manner that not only responds effectively to the diversity present, but also respects our particular history, the complexity of who we are? We turn now to a consideration of different parish models of cultural integration.

Parish Models of Cultural Integration[9] and the Implications for Pastoral Councils

For Catholics, the parish remains the primary place where we encounter the church. Effective parishes provide a context in which our faith can be nurtured and lived out. One determinate of the effectiveness of a parish is the way it is organized and structured. Below are five parish models of cultural integration originally conceived by Rev. Frank Colborn, which I have amended slightly. Rev. Colborn developed these models as he reflected on his pastoral ministry experience with East Los Angeles Hispanics. These parishes are described as (1) the Americanizing parish; (2) the ethnic or national parish; (3) the missionary parish; (4) the parallel parish; (5) the interrelated parish.[10]

The Americanizing Parish

The Americanizing parish is one in which the pastor and pastoral council members understand the role of the parish to be that of assisting all people of color, including recent immigrants, to conform to the historical norm of the parish, to assimilate into the way things have always been done. The role of the parish in assisting its faithful to turn to the gospel is confused with assisting its parishioners to adopt more fully a U.S. life-style. Since newcomers will not advance socially and economically until they learn standard English and adapt themselves to the U.S. culture, those espousing this model believe that the church's mission is best lived out by ensuring that these newcomers have a mainstream U.S. experience of church. Assimilation or "Americanization" is, in effect, more important than evangelization.[11] One rationale for this model is that a diversity of faith expressions creates too much chaos, that the church loses her identity if she allows too much latitude. Building on this is the belief that since throughout the past two millennia the church was significantly shaped by, and was immensely influential in, the development of Western civilization, to a large extent in embracing Catholicism one embraces its Western cultural expressions as they are currently defined by Western European Catholicism and by the predominant U.S. church. Other expressions of Catholicism are considered marginal and therefore less valid.

Typically, pastors and pastoral councils within this model will be made up of individuals who function effectively within the U.S. norm of organization and meeting structure. Pastoral councils, consequently, will attract members who work well within these parameters. While people of color are invited to serve as council members, they do so with the expectation that they will accept these historical norms and methods of operating. Pastoral council members are not expected to understand or allow the experience of people of color to shape the direction of the council's work. Within the geographical boundaries of many parishes operating with this model, demographic research will indicate a significantly diverse Catholic population while pastors and council members will insist, "There aren't very many minorities in our parish. We really don't need to be concerned about diversity." Typically, people of color, and immigrants in particular, are ignored and do not feel welcome in this type of parish.

The Ethnic or National Parish

In contrast to the Americanizing parish, the ethnic or national parish is one in which the pastor, and if he has one, his pastoral council, view their goal as the development of a single immigrant group parish which replicates, as much as possible, the typical parish in the immigrants' parish of origin. The pastor of this type of parish is someone who is an immigrant himself, and therefore someone who speaks the language, who knows the customs and practices of the ethnic group. He knows firsthand the specific concerns and stresses of his parish community because he is experiencing them himself.[12] The parishioners typically are first or second generation. By the third generation, meaning the grandchildren of the original immigrants, participation in an ethnic parish usually drops off substantially. The third generation is usually so well adapted to the U.S. life-style that they no longer seek a church experience which replicates that of their grandparents.[13] The role of the parish in this model is to evangelize parishioners in a manner that will reach them most effectively, namely, in their mother tongue, with rites, customs and rituals which are meaningful for them.

Early on in the development of the U.S. Catholic Church, parishes of this type became common. They were created in response to an organized challenge,

> . . . the diversity of Catholics from different language and cultural backgrounds in Europe. Irish Catholicism differed from German Catholicism not only in language but in a variety of customs and practices which had developed in the cultural environment of Ireland rather than Germany. The response to this by the Church in the United States was the national or language parish. . . . Special parishes were created for members of a particular language and cultural background, German or French (and later on, Polish, Italian, Hungarian, Slovak, Ukranian, etc.) . . . As a matter of course, the German priests established German parishes for the Germans, the French did

likewise. Later on . . . others would follow this example. Thus a large diocese of the United States would consist of a mosaic of territorial and national parishes under the jurisdiction of the bishop.[14]

National parishes ensured a continuity of religious faith for immigrants while at the same time providing "a basis for social solidarity and security."[15] Cultural groups and immigrant groups, as a result, moved quickly into the mainstream.[16] While today there are few *de jure* national parishes, many *de facto* such parishes exist. Quite often these communities are numerically large and draw parishioners from an area which includes several territorial parishes.[17]

In an ethnic parish, the existence and purpose of a pastoral council mirrors what is typical in the immigrants' country of origin. Recently, Vietnamese and Korean Catholic immigrants have come to the U.S. along with priests from their countries. In some U.S. dioceses, these immigrants have set up community centers where mass is celebrated and various ministries are organized. In these cases parish pastoral councils are created to mirror their existence in Vietnam or Korea. As such, pastoral councils frequently will find it difficult to understand and, therefore, follow the pastoral council norms of their local U. S. bishop. More than likely, these pastoral councils will function in a manner which differs from other parish communities within the diocese. Ethnic parish pastors and council members may feel a much stronger connection to the local church in their country of origin. This gap is significantly widened if the local diocese does not provide written materials and other resources in the language of the immigrant group.

The Missionary Parish

A missionary parish resembles an ethnic parish except that the pastor and his staff are either white/Western-European Americans or they share the heritage of the ethnic community, but were born and raised in the U.S. In this model, a pastor and staff focus considerable attention on sensitively serving the needs of the immigrant or ethnic community. Commonly, misunderstandings will surface between the pastor and the ethnic community that he serves, which result more from their significant cultural dissonance than from anything else. As a consequence much time, often years, and great patience are needed before there is a genuine comfort level between the community and the pastor and staff. Usually, the pastor and staff find themselves straddling their knowledge of and comfort with a U. S. church experience and, the immigrant or ethnic community's perceptions and expectations of church.[18]

Pastoral council members in parishes which employ the missionary model will find themselves at the heart of the cultural dissonance, caught somewhere between a U.S. interpretation of what it means to be a parish community and the resulting vision of parish leadership, and their experience of church in their country of origin. In this model pastoral councils have the potential to be sources of both immense creativity and immense frustration.

The Parallel Parish

In a parallel parish, the pastor and parish staff respond to the ministerial needs of each cultural group in isolation from the rest.[19] "Each cultural or linguistic group will have its own organizations, its own services, perhaps even its own priest assigned to serve just that group. . . . The result is, in a sense, the existence within the same parish boundaries of two "ethnic" parishes, who happen to use the same church buildings." [20] Each cultural group typically represents a sizable portion of the parish. In this model the pastor and staff believe that the role of the parish is to respond to each of the major ethnic groups individually in a manner which is effective for them. In a time of limited priest personnel, of limited financial resources, and of parish facilities which are not fully occupied, many dioceses have chosen to use this model in responding to the needs of cultural groups. In addition, many feel that this model, in a limited fashion and the next model to a greater extent, offer parishes an opportunity to realize to some degree that it means to be a world church. On an ongoing basis, parishes employing these models will face a wide range of questions which arise from attempting to respond to a culturally diverse community. Sometimes parallel parishes choose to celebrate bilingual or multilingual masses, particularly during Christmas and Holy Week. This is usually done so that the celebrant will have a somewhat manageable schedule. While scheduling these liturgical experiences makes a lot of practical sense, parishioners may not be satisfied with these experiences if this is the only time the various cultural groups gather as one parish community. Liturgy, if it is effective, enables us to draw closer to God and each other. As such, liturgy is an experience of intimacy and is more meaningfully shared after the parish community has come together for other experiences of parish life.

Unfortunately, the ministerial needs of the community(ies) of color often are considered second when it comes to hiring parish staff members, scheduling the use of parish facilities, of parish office space, of church space for mass, etc. Practices such as these can impede the pastor and pastoral council's efforts to foster the values of mutuality and partnership among different cultural groups within the parish. Moreover, such practices can breed mistrust, and thereby encourage stereotypes and prejudices to deepen.

The pastoral council in a parallel parish can be organized in different ways. One option is for the pastor and his staff to have a group of pastoral advisors for each cultural group which focuses on the needs of its own group. This allows the individual cultural group to maintain a healthy and strong sense of their own identity, therefore enabling them to more effectively integrate with the wider parish community. True integration always takes place from a point of strength and not in isolation. From representatives of each group of pastoral advisors, the pastor can create a pastoral council which truly represents the whole parish community. One other advantage to this model is that it respects the organizing patterns and leadership models of each cultural group rather than attempting to create a single group which may function in a manner which is unknown to many of its members. Another more common option is for pastoral councils to be selected through a process which results in an almost exclusively white/Western-European American council. After which the pastor appoints a representative from each of the remaining cultural and/or linguistic groups. This option inevitably breeds mistrust, frustration and the perception of tokenism.

The Interrelated Parish

The interrelated parish is one in which the pastor and staff respond to the ministerial needs of all the cultural groups in a manner which respects their particular culture while inviting them to share the richness of their culture with the other cultural groups.[21] The assumption of leadership in this model is that the ultimate goal of our de facto culturally diverse parishes is to invite parishioners into a space where they can appreciate and celebrate the ethnic diversity which is our church. Parishes which have adopted this model are extremely rare. Almost always such parishes have a pastor and staff who are deeply committed to a global vision of the church. All the parish staff members need to understand that they are to be at the service of all parishioners. While they may serve one cultural group more often than the others, they do cross over cultural boundaries.[22] Large numbers of bilingual and bicultural parishioners are also important. These individuals act as bridge builders between parishioners who are monolingual and who identify exclusively with one of the parish's cultural groups. Frequently, this type of parish is one that evolves after many years, and even generations, with two or more cultural groups identifying with the parish. Resources in this parish are distributed proportional to the numbers present of each cultural group. Parishioners in this model view their parish as a community of communities.

The pastoral council in this model may be organized similar to the options discussed in the parallel parish model. Or the pastoral council may be made up of a few leaders from each cultural group proportional to their numbers in the parish. Such a council has the potential to become a symbol of unity for the wider parish community. If they are able to work together effectively, the council can be in a position to greatly and positively contribute a harmonious vision of cultural diversity to the parish and its surrounding neighborhood. This structure presents some challenges. Often representatives of the different ethnic communities do not share a common language. Even if everyone speaks some English, those for whom it is not their first language can feel limited in their ability to effectively express the needs of their own people. Bi- or multilingual meetings are an option, but can be cumbersome. In addition, there will be significant cultural differences in expectations about how a council will interpret and live out its purpose.

Ownership

These five models provide a lens through which pastors and pastoral council members can clarify their experience of cultural integration. Many parishes may not be exclusively one model or the other. Often parishes will find themselves to be a combination of an ethnic and a missionary parish or a parallel and interrelated parish. Regardless of the model or models which fit the situation of a particular parish community, the underlying issue is that of ownership.

The question of **ownership** resides at the heart of our discussion of parish models of cultural integration. Who is making decisions in the parish about how resources will be distributed? To whom does the parish belong? All of us want and need to be able to shape our future, to have a space which we recognize as our own. Pastors, with the assistance of pastoral council members and parish staff members essentially define how parishes will respond to the question of **ownership.**

For many communities of color, survival is an overriding question—survival both physically and socioculturally. Because communities of color have felt silences, invisible and marginated by U. S. society at large and frequently by the church as well, the notion of "survival" shapes participation in the parishes, particularly in any type of leadership role.

> Survival has to do with more than barely living. Survival has to do with the struggle to be fully living. To survive, one has to have "the power to decide about one's history and one's vocation or historical mission." This translates into two sets of questions: questions about physical survival and questions about cultural historical survival. Though these two aspects of survival are closely linked in many given situations, they are not identical.[23]

The question of cultural-historical survival is overriding because frequently our ethnic communities live, work and worship in an environment that is foreign. In part, the experience of foreignness is rooted in history. History defines for us that which is meaningful, that which is important to know, to remember. History is almost always retold from the experience of the "winners" which leaves communities of color in a historical, cultural wasteland in which their experience is only affirmed and validated within their own cultural community, but is not held up as significant for the wider church community. The result is a continual experience of being second, of being a guest in someone else's home, of being unidentifiable, unknown, unrecognized. An understanding and appreciation of this phenomenon is critical to the creation of an authentically inclusive pastoral council.

In summary, all parishes find themselves somewhere along the cultural integration continuum. The Americanizing parish sits at one end of the continuum, assimilation, while the ethnic or national parish sit at the other end, segregation. The remaining three parish models represent points somewhere in between. Many parish communities attempt to emulate one of the middle three parish models, all of which tend to be more complex and therefore present a greater challenge. Each of them attempts to foster a respect for distinct cultural expressions within a greater whole. Some parishes review their history and will find that the model which fits where they are now is different from the model which fit ten years ago. Some may begin as an Americanizing parish, continue as a parallel parish and, finally, become an interrelated parish.[24] Pastors and pastoral council members would do well to discuss where they are situated along the continuum and the benefits and limitations of their choice. In parishes where not much thought is given or gratitude felt for the gift and challenge of cultural diversity, pastoral councils can be inclined to assume a white/Western-European American bias which tends to eliminate any meaningful participation of African-Americans, Asian/Pacific Islanders, Latinos or Native Americans.

Reflection Questions

1) Which of the models does your parish resemble? Does this model respond well to the needs of your parish community? Why?

2) Review the past ten years of your parish community's history. How has the ethnic diversity changed during the past ten years?

3) What will be the ethnic makeup of your parish five years from now? Ten years from now?

4) How has your pastoral council responded to the ethnic diversity of your parish?

5) What is the church's task in the face of cultural diversity?

Challenges and Signs of Hope

Our focus now turns to some of the challenges in attempting to create a pastoral council which genuinely reflects cultural diversity. Four interrelated challenges stand out: the perduring and historical relationship of Christianity to Western civilization, the perceived role of the church in U.S. society, the socioeconomic gap between middle and lower income parishioners and, finally, the internalization of racism.

While the Christian message is not solely tied to any one culture, and therefore is inherently open to all cultures, for the past two millennia Christianity has shaped and been shaped by Western civilization. The gospel and our experience of church, has been presented historically in a "Western package." This begs the question: "Is it possible for cultural groups to extract the essentials of Christianity and allow them to evangelize their culture?" Can the gospel call non-Western cultures to a genuine conversion without forcing on them strange symbols, systems and social practices?[25] Compounding this concern is an attitude of Western cultural superiority which is typically promoted by various institutions and systems within the U. S. The California legislature's successful attempt to pass an "English Only" law is one example. The history and literature texts which have been used by many school systems in the U.S. are another example. While recently there has been much improvement in this area, historically school textbooks have illustrated an overwhelming Western bias.

This bias has significantly influenced our church as well. To-day a significant percentage of our U.S. church is Hispanic, yet church leadership across the country does not reflect this reality. Nor are proportionate numbers of other communities of color represented in positions of church leadership. The critical factor has to do with the power that members of the predominant U.S. cultural group have to institutionalize their notion of superiority through the control of the church's direction and resource allocation. Pastors and parish council members need to grapple with whether or not they are willing to let go, to invite others as full partners into the process of shaping the future of the parish, the future of the local church.

A second related challenge focuses on the vision of the pastor and parish pastoral council members as they consider the role of the church in the U.S. Is the church's primary role to assist immigrants and other people of color to become "Americans," to adapt to the mainstream of U.S. culture? Or, is the church called to evangelize its faithful in a manner which respects their culture? This is a constant concern in parishes. Often one hears parishioners ask: "Why can't you folks learn English? After all you have been here fifteen years? Why do you people insist on being different? You are welcome to come to our masses. When will you all become 'Americans?' " In many respects the church's ability to address and overcome this challenge is dependent upon the pastor's and the parish pastoral council members' ability to distinguish between religious values and U.S. cultural values.

Thus, many communities of color do not look to parish life as the sole or even primary source of their Catholic identity. Frequently various apostolic movements are much more effective at feeding and nurturing Catholic identity and spirituality for people of color. Often people of color will organize and lead these movements within their own cultural group, thus creating a climate in which both religious and cultural identity is recognized and deepened.[26] Such movements include the Kateri Tekakwitha Circles, Cursillos, Knights and Ladies of Peter Claver, Marriage Encounter, Legion of Mary, etc.

A third and extremely difficult challenge is that of socioeconomic class. Typically the pastor and pastoral council members come out of a different socioeconomic context than that of many people of color. While there are many exceptions, people of color are largely poor and the leadership in most U.S. parishes tends to be socially and economically middle class.

> Bridging the gap between middle class and poor is more difficult than bridging the gap between cultures. In a sense poor people tend to create a cultural style of their own in response to the problems of survival; this is particularly true when the poor are in the presence of a middle-class population.[27]

This challenge can make diversity on the pastoral council very hard to achieve.

And finally, a fourth challenge: the role of racism in the lives of people of color. While there are many external racial barriers which people of color experience, perhaps the most devastating and oppressive ones are those which live within. Frequently, racial barriers become internalized over the course of the first half of life and therefore shape the individual's imagination regarding what is possible. This works sharply against the possibility that individuals from communities of color, and women in particular, will step forward and offer themselves for positions of leadership in the parish. For those who do step forward, especially if they are the only representative on the council from their ethnic group, the experience of membership can be one of frustration and anger. They will likely experience the cultural dissonance of the group more sharply than others.

Daunting as these challenges may be, we are called to be people of hope. Signs of hope can be found in our society at large, in the church, and finally in the efforts of many people of color.

Within our society there is much that is moving us closer to one another. In the U.S. and around the world, many speak of our becoming a "global village." The informational and technological advances of recent years have created a strong sense of interrelatedness and interdependency. Adding to that, as white/Western-

European American women [28] enter the workforce in ever increasing numbers, many of them advance a vision of a greater equality for women in the workplace and in public life. While focused on gender, in some cases this vision breaks the ground for a fuller consideration of race and culture. All the "isms," (racism, sexism, classism, ageism, etc.) are rooted in a social system of dualisms. One group considers itself superior to another. Any attempt to develop a social system based on partnership and inclusion ultimately must address the concerns of all excluded groups. In the business world, management theorists are suggesting a more serious consideration of consultation in the decision making process. Again, this is one more expression of our interdependency.

In the church there are also many signs of hope. The emergence and efforts of parish pastoral councils since the early 1970s are a sign of hope. The consultative process[29] which is at the heart of the council's work can, if lived out fully, acknowledge interdependency and hold open the possibility of inclusion. The consultative process and the selection process for pastoral council membership, present excellent opportunities for the council to take seriously the cultural diversity of the parish community. Secondly, the U.S. church is in many ways in a time of strained resources: the number of clergy are declining, the finances of many dioceses and parishes are stretched to the limit. At first glance this feels more stressful than hopeful, but it does present us with an important opportunity. In a time of strained resources we are compelled to depend on one another and to think creatively. Times such as these build community. We find that we need one another. And, finally, there is a desire and commitment on the part of many in leadership to support "the coming-to-be of a world-church."[30] Many pastoral council members, parish staff members, pastors and bishops sincerely want to embrace cultural diversity, to consider more fully what it means to be catholic, to be universal.

Finally, a growing awareness is emerging among Catholic parishioners of color of the need to lead our own communities, to act on our own behalf. This awareness has been fostered through the Encuentro process and the subsequent development of a National Plan for Hispanic Ministry, through the Congress process for African-American Catholics; through the Tekakwitha conference for Native American Catholics; and through many, many conferences in which Asian and Pacific Islander Catholics have developed their own pastoral plans for ministry. In addition, in many cities across the country community organizations based in our churches are developing the leadership abilities of Catholic parishioners of color, thereby enabling them to take an active role in their parishes and in public life. The Industrial Areas Foundation[31] is one such network which has had a profound impact on Catholic parishioners, including many people of color, in communities across the states of Texas, New Mexico, Arizona and California. This network has developed strong organizations in other parts of the country as well.

After considering some of the challenges and some of the signs of hope, what might a culturally integrated parish look like?

Characteristics of a Culturally Integrated Parish

There are a few characteristics which are important for a committed pastor and pastoral council to foster and encourage if they are to create a community which takes seriously the call both to evangelize and to be an inclusive parish community, a global church. First of all, the parish community would need to be "accepting and willing to build a strong inner unity of faith upon a loose diversity of cultural features and expression."[32] Each cultural group would be free to develop and model its particular faith expressions without pressing them on other cultural groups. Secondly, each cultural group would need to "respectfully share within the universal Church the variety of their social practice and symbolism as a result of the contact between their underlying meanings, values and patterns and the recognized central meanings and values of the Christian message."[33] Third, each cultural group would need to be committed to the challenge of evangelization. In a spirit of care and discernment, members of each cultural group would engage in a critical assessment of their own culture in light of the Christian message.[34] Fourth, through their process of discernment, each cultural group would put aside cultural interpretations and values which were genuinely perceived to be incompatible with the Christian message. Fifth, in light of the Christian message, each cultural group would discover more fully the ultimate meaning of their culture, the native genius of their particular interpretation of humanity. And finally, confident in the gift of their own identity and future as a people, each cultural group "would be open to exchange their riches with other cultures, while at the same time remaining faithful to their own genius."[35] These characteristics describe an ideal to be sought in parishes; they can provoke us to imagine our parishes differently, to imagine them more inclusively.

Conclusion

The symbol of Pentecost (Acts 2:4–11) provides a prophetic lens through which we can peer into the future. Pentecost points to a future of cultural pluralism, to "the coming-to-be of a world-Church."[36] In Pentecost we see both a respect for and yet a harmonizing of differences.

The arch of history that bends toward justice, bends in the direction of Pentecost. Perhaps our call as pastoral council members is best summed up in the words of Robert McAfee Brown:

There must not only be a vision of the global family, but a sufficient sense of belonging to the global family so people will undertake risks on behalf of that broad family. (NCR, April 8, 1977)

Notes

[1] Many individuals who work within the Archdiocese of Seattle assisted me with the development of this chapter. I would like to acknowledge them and offer my thanks: Mary Beth Celio, Patti Falsetto, Richard Hayatsu, Veronica Leasioloagi-Barber, Joseph McGowan, Sharon Pitre-Williams, Dennis O'Leary, Patty Repikoff and Ed Williams.

[2] Karl Rahner, SJ, "Towards a Fundamental Theological Interpretation of Vatican II," *Theological Studies* 40 (December, 1979), p. 717.

[3] Regis Duffy, OFM, *Real Presence: Worship, Sacraments and Commitment* (San Francisco: Harper and Row, 1982), p. 3.

⁴Azevedo, p. 9.

⁵Frank Ponce, "Enculturation in the U.S. Catholic Church: A Vision and Some Pastoral Implications," *New Catholic World,* July/August, 1980, 166.

⁶Pope Paul VI, *Evangelii Nutiandi, On Evangelization in the Modern World* (Washington, D.C.: United States Catholic Conference, 1976).

⁷Ibid, no. 20.

⁸There are many other documents which pastoral council members may want to consider studying. The following is a list of some of them. (1) Pontifical Commission "Justitia Et Pax." *The Church and Racism: Towards a More Fraternal Society.* Washington, D.C.: USCC, 1988. (2) National Conference of Catholic Bishops. "Brothers and Sisters to Us," Pastoral Letter on Racism. *Origins,* Vol. 9, No. 24, November 29, 1979. (3) National Conference of Catholic Bishops, *Hispanic Presence: Challenge and Commitment,* Washington, D.C.: USCC, 1983. (4) U.S. Bishops' Committee for Social Development and World Peace. "Beyond the Melting Pot, Cultural Pluralism in the United States, *Origins,* Vol. 10, No. 31, January 15, 1981. (5) *Vatican Council II,* ed., Austin Flannery, O.P. (Northport, N.Y.: Costello Publishing Co., 1992).

⁹Rev. Frank Colborn has written an unpublished manuscript entitled Reflections on Pastoral Ministry among Hispanics. In the section "Pastoral Ministry: Cultural Integration," he reflects on five distinct parish models of cultural integration (pp. 19–23). Allan Figueroa Deck, SJ, *The Second Wave: Hispanic Ministry and the Evangelization of Cultures* (Mahwah, N.J.: Paulist Press, 1989), p. 61.

¹⁰ Deck, p. 61.

¹¹ Ibid.

¹² Ibid.

¹³ Joseph P. Fitzpatrick, SJ, *One Church Many Cultures: The Challenge of Diversity* (Kansas City, Mo.: Sheed and Ward, 1987), p. 105

¹⁴ Fitzpatrick, p. 103

¹⁵ Ibid, p. 116

¹⁶ Ibid.

¹⁷ Deck, p. 62

[18] Ibid.

[19] Ibid.

[20] Colborn, p. 21

[21] Deck, p. 63

[22] Colborn, p. 21

[23] Ada Maria Isasi-Diaz and Yolanda Tarrango, *Hispanic Women: Prophetic Voice in the Church* (San Francisco: Harper & Row, 1988), p 4.

[24] Colborn, p. 21

[25] Azevedo, p. 25

[26] Deck, p. 63

[27] Fitzpatrick, p. 141

[28] I do not include women of color in highlighting this social shift since for the overwhelming majority of them, their participation in the workforce long predates this most recent transition.

[29] By the term "consultative process" I mean a comprehensive and systematic listening process which engages all sectors of the parish community in expressing their hopes and needs.

[30] Karl Rahner, SJ, "Basic Theological Interpretation of the Second Vatican Council," *Theological Investigations,* Vol. XX, "Concern for the Church." (New York: Crossroad 1981) p. 82

[31] The Industrial Areas Foundation was founded based on the work of Saul Alinsky in the early part of this century.

[32] Azevedo, p. 27

[33] Ibid.

[34] Ibid.

[35] Ibid, p. 28

[36] Rahner, p. 82

Strategic/Pastoral Planning

by Arthur X. Deegan II, Ph.D.

Earlier chapters have explained pastoral planning as a process employing a variety of skills, specifically those involved in organization development, systems design, research and theological reflection. As might have been expected, it can be said that the pastoral planner, therefore, borrows some techniques from secular sciences and overlays them with a theological coloring to carry out the work of the church.

That being the case, when it comes time to understand some of the mechanics and to actually "do" pastoral planning, a good place to start is with those social science disciplines. This often has the result of reminding pastoral council members of some of the techniques they see used about them in workaday situations—old friends, as it were—which simply have to be put to work in a church environment. One such process used by those engaged in planning in a wide variety of professions is strategic planning. The purpose of this chapter is to define strategic planning and explain the typical steps in this process in a way that they can be applied to pastoral planning in a parish context.

Strategic Planning Defined

The word "strategic" comes from the Greek "stratos" meaning "army" and "ego" meaning "leader." As an adjective, it therefore means "pertaining to the leader of an army, or a general." People who do strategic things are those in charge of an operation, usually the chief executive. We are immediately in the domain of those who are accountable for the entire mission, the leader(s). Our vantage point permits envisioning the broadest possible scope, the longest lasting effects.

The focus of the leadership group is on the most significant items, which introduces the concept of prioritizing, another important element in understanding what strategizing is all about. Strategic things cannot afford to get bogged down in minutiae, which we must quickly say is not the same as saying we will avoid details: it's the *insignificant* details that cause the trouble sometimes and distract the leadership attention from more important considerations.

"Planning" is the process of looking to the future, selecting a desired outcome and charting a roadmap to achieve that destination. When we combine the words "strategic" and "planning" we can define the process thus:

Strategic planning is the formulation of long-term objectives for an organization and the selection of significant methodologies to achieve those objectives in light of an uncertain environment in which it must operate.

You will note the final section of that definition adds yet another important element in the planning of successful generals: recognizing that as you attempt to guide your army to its objectives, you must always be mindful of opposing forces (or friendly forces) which may cause you to take this or that action in response. You don't operate in a vacuum; your environment has a lot to do with your eventual success, and that environment is not always something you can correctly anticipate, much less control to your own liking. Hence, an "uncertain environment."

The essence of strategic planning is to provide the conceptual framework for the organization's "general"/chief executive and other leaders which will enable them to make day-to-day decisions that will affect the likelihood of the group's ever fulfilling its mission. The strategic planning problem becomes one of choosing among alternative strategies in light of varying assumptions about the organization and its environment, which is always characterized by a high degree of risk and uncertainty.

If this approach is applied to planning in the church (pastoral planning), then the overarching concern will be the mission of the parish as enunciated by its leadership. Mission is the principle for organizing ALL church efforts. It will be a prayerful and participative process by which members acknowledge their purpose, their goals, and their priorities, then devise accountable ways to ensure realization of their pastoral plan.

The pastoral plan will have to be comprehensive in scope—encompassing all the important facets of church life: worship, education, service and administration. Just as the general wishes to apply his logistics (resources) in order to have the greatest impact in carrying out the plan, the parish leadership will use pastoral planning as an essential ingredient of good stewardship. Its purpose will be to facilitate and guide decision making so that scarce resources are applied to meeting the changing situations in our society and the emerging needs of people.

A Dynamic Process

Figure 1 will serve to suggest a chronology of steps to devise a strategic/pastoral plan. (After enumerating the steps and suggesting the logic in their stated sequence, we shall return to a discussion of each one of the steps.)

1. The parish begins by identifying its MISSION. This is a brief statement which describes a destination, a desired position in the future: what we want to be (or be like) some time in the future. Usually a 3 to 5 year time horizon is far enough in the future; things get rather fuzzy much beyond that.

2. Recognizing that the surroundings of the parish (called here its environment) will color its ability to develop in the future, parish leaders conduct an ENVIRONMENTAL ASSESSMENT, an examination of the most likely trends forecast in certain significant areas, and the possible implications (both positive and negative) of those trends on the life of the parish in the future.

3. Having established a desired position in the future and assessed the pluses and minuses of forces to be encountered, the parish then takes stock of its present ability to cope with such a scenario: it does a SWOTs ANALYSIS. That is, it makes a list of Strengths, Weaknesses, Opportunities and Threats, to judge

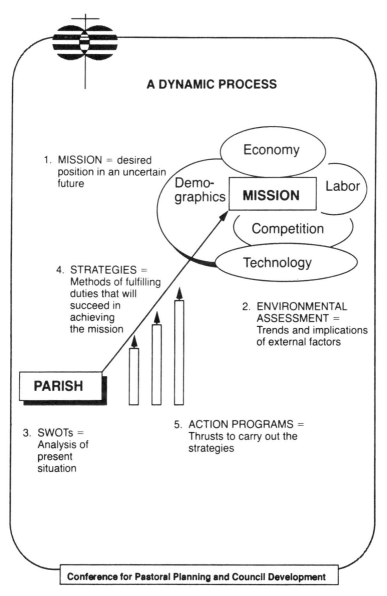

Figure 1

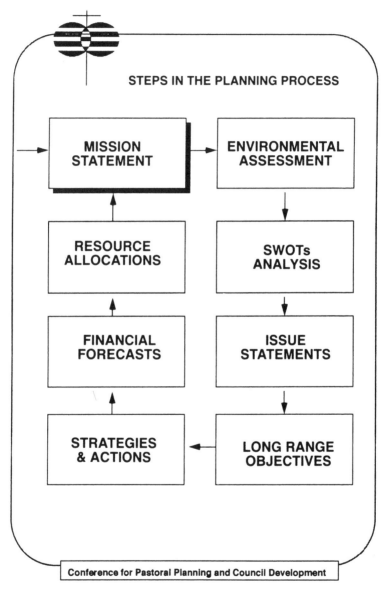

Figure 2

whether it has the wherewithal to undertake the challenge presented by the future.

4. In order to get from where we are to where we want to be we set LONG RANGE OBJECTIVES and STRATEGIES. These are intermediate goals on the road to our ultimate mission; they are measurable results we target as milestones or phases in completing our plan. They are general directions we want to pursue to keep us aimed at our destiny. They are methods of fulfilling duties that will succeed in achieving the mission.

5. The path from where the parish is at the present and where it wants to be in the future is the real measure of the challenge it faces. That path may be a steep incline, or it may be a less arduous uphill climb. Hopefully it will never have a negative slope (a line pointing downward). To keep the parish constantly "on track" toward its mission, the general direction line must be buttressed every so often with supports, labeled here ACTION PROGRAMS, or thrusts to carry out the strategies.

Figure 2 is a more familiar flow chart indicating the typical steps in the strategic planning process. We will now take each of these in turn and suggest how they might be carried out as part of a parish strategic/pastoral planning process.

The Mission Statement

The **purpose** of a mission statement is to answer some fundamental questions: Why are we here? What do we hope to become? What is our purpose? What are we called to be? What do we believe in? What are our values?

There is no one format for a mission statement. Some prefer a very simple sentence that can be committed to memory as a description of the basic purpose of the group. Others include in the mission a list of the values and commitments to stakeholders (a term we shall define a little later). Still others divide it into Vision, Philosophy and Role.

Here is an example of a diocesan mission statement:

**The mission of
the Diocese of** _____

is the continuation of
Christ's mission in this locale,
in order to become
what we are called to be:
a Catholic Faith community,
dedicated:
to be a sign to men and women
of a gospel-living people,
and to give service to all
through proclaiming the word
and celebrating the sacraments.

Here is a sample of parish mission statement:

As a parish, which is united with the Catholic Church
throughout the world, we the people of _____
Parish proclaim our belief in the message and mission of
Jesus Christ.

As a parish, we seek to live out that belief as a community
of worship, of shared faith and of service where each member shares with others the gifts and talents received from
God.

You **use** a mission statement as a logo: it tells people what you
stand for, what you're committed to and drives all subsequent
decisions. In effect, members intend to relate all actions to the
realization of the vision it contains. The mission statement is publi-
cized and distributed widely. A copy is often included in official
documents (annual reports and the like). Sometimes it is repro-
duced on wallet size cards and carried on one's person.

A practical exercise to assist pastoral council members in the
writing of a mission statement consists of the following two steps.

Step One: Review the five models of church described by Fr.
Avery Dulles, SJ.[1] Ask each person to write down one or two
sentences in answer to this question: "Which aspect(s) of church
have you experienced most in this parish? How so?" Then ask
them to write one or two sentences in answer to this second ques-

tion: "Which aspect of church life needs to be strengthened? Why?"

Step Two: Ask various individuals to share their answers to the two questions in Step One. Try to form a consensus from the ensuing discussion in order to compile a list of value statements to make up your mission statement.

NOTE: The words and phrases used in a mission statement are usually broad and non-specific. The mission is not a goal. Goals are specific and measurable results which you intend to accomplish. They will have an endpoint. The mission, however, is what you will always be aiming at, but not ever quite reaching. The mission describes what you hope to become. You will forever be in a state of "becoming," which is why our journey is described as a perpetual pilgrimage.

Environmental Assessment

With a clear understanding of what the parish wishes to become, you now turn your attention to those factors which will help or hinder the process. The parish does not exist in a vacuum; it is very much affected by its surroundings. You will want to examine carefully what the trends are in some of the more influential factors and consider their possible implications on your success or failure in carrying out the mission.

The *demographics* of the parish and its surrounding community will have a major influence on the future of the parish. What are the trends with regard to the number of families? the number and age of their members? their socioeconomic status? their ethnic, racial and cultural heritage? Is the parish still growing or is it built out? Are people leaving the area in great numbers? Has a major employer cut back or moved away? Is some major development (a new subdivision, a shopping mall, a new expressway) about to change the makeup of the parish population?

The general *economy* of the community at large has a bearing on your ability to carry out the mission. What is happening to unemployment, to interest rates, to investment opportunities, to the availability of capital, to wage rates, to inflation, to the national and local debt? What will all this mean to the giving habits of people, to the cost of construction, to parish salary costs, to the timing of capital improvements, to tuition?

Advances in *technology* should also be assessed in terms of impact on the mission of the parish. How could the parish make use of the latest developments in communication technology, in educational equipment, in construction, in maintenance, in computerization?

Conditions in the *labor market* may also have a bearing on your mission. Consider carefully the trends with regard to the availability of active and retired priests, religious educators, music directors, teachers, custodians, secretarial personnel. Note what is happening to wages, health insurance and other benefits, payroll taxes and their cost to the parish.

Competition for the time and allegiance of adults and youth alike is another important consideration. Are other denominational churches nearby becoming more attractive to your parishioners? Are some of your people finding neighboring Catholic parishes more "user-friendly"? How are you being impacted by TV, sports programs, movies, and other assorted cultural and/or recreational pursuits?

A final environmental factor to consider deals with trends in *government,* both church and civil. What laws are pending? What new regulations are in the offing? How will they affect carrying out your mission?

SWOTs Analysis

The next logical question to ask yourselves is: Given the challenge of all these environmental factors impacting our desire to carry out our mission, how well prepared are we to cope? What chance do we have to succeed?

You answer questions like that by doing a self-analysis, by looking at the parish's internal strengths and weaknesses, and its external opportunities and threats. It should immediately be noted that words like "strength" and "weakness" are relative terms. To judge whether a given phenomenon is either a plus or a minus requires some criteria, some absolute, against which to assess it.

That absolute is the mission statement. Something will be either an asset or a liability in terms of its being able to contribute to the mission.

The best way to do this self-analysis is to ask each person on the pastoral council to list some arbitrary number (say 3 or 4) of strengths, weaknesses, opportunities and threats, and then to simply brainstorm with the group to make a consolidated list. It will be important to agree on definitions ahead of time, such as the following:

An internal STRENGTH is some asset, resources, success which can best be used to build upon in achieving the mission.

An internal WEAKNESS is some need, failing, inadequacy or deficiency which can hinder the achieving of the mission.

An external OPPORTUNITY is something positive outside the parish which has not yet been adequately made use of in achieving the mission.

An external THREAT is some obstacle able to seriously impede the achievement of the mission.

Needs Analysis or Stakeholder Analysis

Our discussion has envisioned the pastoral council as a group to do this strategic/pastoral planning. The point was made that this is the planning that the leader(s) cannot delegate to others. Nonetheless, the council might wish to have input from others. Two most common alternative methods for gaining this input are a formal needs analysis, or a briefer stakeholder analysis.

Because strategic planning is the way you are "reading the signs of the times" and "meeting the needs of the times," it involves some method or other of identifying current needs of the people you are trying to serve. The SWOTs analysis step is one way of doing that. There are numerous other ways of bringing to light the particular needs of the parish at the moment. A survey instrument could be devised and administered to the entire parish membership or a representative sample of the parishioners. Focus groups could be formed to brainstorm some of the same topics. Polling could be done. "Town hall" meetings could be held to which is invited anyone with a contribution to make. The formulation of questionnaires and the techniques for extracting useful information from groups are the subjects of entire books themselves. Suffice it to say here that any professional approach to providing input for the leadership to consider in assessing where the parish is at the present time can be useful at this stage of the planning process.

Stakeholder analysis is a term used to suggest that any attempt to identify needs should be careful not to exclude any persons or groups who have a legitimate stake in what the parish is planning. Such persons would include registered members of the parish, non-registered members of the parish (the pastor is responsible for all souls included in the boundaries of his parish), "fallen away" or non-practicing Catholics, the unchurched, others living in the community, parish staff, vendors and suppliers, lenders and grantors, the bishop and chancery staff, and so on.

Representatives from some of these major groups can be identified and asked to complete a survey or just to nominate strengths and weaknesses of the parish. Their answers are then used by the pastoral council members as a check against their own view of the current state of affairs in the parish.

Key Issue Analysis

Up to this point the group has been doing some serious soul searching. Much information has been arrayed to situate the parish—where it is now and where it wants to be in the future. Typically much will have been discussed to get some feel of the scope of the job ahead. It is time now to summarize this situational analysis and begin to decide what to do about it all. This is often called simply the identification of key issues.

In several areas, there should by now be an appreciation of being at one level presently, with a desire to be at another level some time in the future. The difference between these two levels can be considered a "gap." Because strategic/pastoral planning must always be involved with the high priority issues, the group should now sift through all the "gaps" that have been identified and try to zero in on the most significant. There is no arbitrary number here as at other points in this process, but a rough rule of thumb might be to try to limit your concentration to 3 or 4 major issues.

At the same time, the analysis to date must also have identified some areas where there is no gap, but rather a desire to continue doing well what is of great service already. The "issue" in this case will be how to maintain such centers of excellence. Another 1 or 2 such issues should be identified.

It is often useful at this point for someone to prepare a brief "issue paper" for each of the key issues thus identified. Such a brief (2 page) paper could be constructed following this outline:

1. Statement of the issue (framed as a question needing an answer). For example, "What services should we be providing the growing number of Hispanic parishioners?"
2. Description of the present situation. (Why is it a major issue?) For example, cite the demographic figures and mention that Spanish-speaking newcomers to the area are being won over by other denominations by the provision of daycare services and the ministry of a Spanish-speaking minister.
3. Description of the desired situation. (This will become an objective.) For example, having regularly scheduled mass in Spanish and religious education classes for their youngsters.
4. Discussion of promoting forces—things that will help resolve the issue. For example, the recent ordination locally of a Spanish-speaking priest and a new parishioner who teaches English to Spanish-speaking adults.
5. Discussion of blocking forces—things now hindering resolution of the issue. For example, the absence of any real leader among the new Hispanics.
6. Specific recommendations; try to offer several alternatives.
7. Estimated costs (in personnel and dollars) to implement suggestions.

The group can then discuss each of the issue papers for the purpose of coming to a consensus about their relative importance, and about which recommendations to adopt.

Long Range Objectives and Strategies

For each of the issues discussed, the pastoral council will want to select a measurable objective (goal) describing the desired situation some time in the future. Notice the attaining of the desired result is what is long range. The steps to begin to get there may happen overnight. The belief that tomorrow's actions will have a long-term result is what makes them strategic, not the fact that it might take a long time to implement the associated actions.

There can be more than one objective dealing with each issue, but the number of them is not the important thing: choosing *realistic* objectives is what is needed. To support each objective, you will want to get agreement on:

- its relative priority, even if expressed simply as high, medium or low in comparison with the other objectives;
- some person or committee of the council to have oversight responsibility for the objective;
- the names of others who will be expected to provide support in reaching the objective;
- a target date for the completion of the objective;
- an itemization of the general approach to be used in reaching the objective; note again that these will be generalizations; for example, "update our parish census information in the next 24 months." The specific steps—or "how to"—will follow in the next step.

Actions

Everything up to this point is part of what earlier chapters in this book called visioning or the developmental work of the transitional kind of parish pastoral council evolving today. What follows is the Implementation portion. Someone has to *do* something to implement the strategies outlined above. The council should still be involved in discussing those actions, but the *execution* of those actions is best left up to parish staff.

This part of the plan calls for discussion and agreement on the individual steps to be taken to implement the general strategies selected for each objective. For example, in order to update parish census information, it may be appropriate to conduct an entirely new census, or it may be necessary only to obtain more recent information since the last census. Even then, there are several ways to do either of those: in person, by phone, by mail, etc.

This part is really not any different from program planning that has been going on in the past, but strategic planning brings a new discipline to the process by focusing such action plans on high priority strategies in pursuit of a clearly enunciated mission. Everything must flow from the mission and be geared to promoting the mission values. Since staff (and volunteers) will be carrying out the actions, this process insures that their energies will be spent in pursuit of those issues deemed important by the leadership of the parish.

While not anything startlingly new, this step is nonetheless extremely important as far as implementing the plan is concerned. Without some concrete steps to put the plan into action, it will remain a fond dream, another volume on a shelf gathering dust. Therefore, it is important that individuals accept the work involved in carrying out these actions, and make commitments to report back on their progress periodically.

Resource Allocations

It will also be important that sufficient resources be made available to those delegated to implement the action steps agreed upon. At times this means freeing someone up from chores which are now seen not to make much of a contribution to the strategic plan. Other times it means one of the first action steps is to get the help needed, either through volunteers or paid staff. In all cases it means that budgeting is an important step to follow what has gone before. You budget in order to implement the plan; you try not to fix a budget and then plan what you can do with those fixed resources.

It is common enough, however, to find that a plan has come up with some wonderful ideas which just are unrealistic in light of available resources. This calls for doing a reality check. We did not want to begin with the budget, lest creativity and enthusiasm be constrained during the planning process, but now that imaginations have been given free rein, the real world requires that budgetary constraints be addressed. It may, therefore, be necessary to back off from some aspects of the plan due to shortage of funds or personnel. But when this is done, at least it is done in full recognition of what the priorities are, and the items labeled "low" in priority earlier can be the first ones to be postponed or rethought.

Conclusion

The process outlined in some detail in this chapter attempts to describe how visioning, prioritizing, and focusing can take place in a parish context. These elements of pastoral planning stem principally from the disciplines of organization development, systems design and research. The spirit which gives life to these secular sciences is theological reflection, which must infuse each step of the process. While no specific reference has been made to it in this discussion, the overriding importance of the mission, which presumably will capture spiritual values, will serve as a reminder that the care of souls must permeate the plan and its implementation.

Note

[1] For a simple explanation of the five models in a manner useful for this exercise, see "Today's Parish—What Should It Be?" by Rev. Joseph M. Champlin, St. Anthony Messenger Press, 1975; *Models of Church,* Avery Dulles, Image Books, Doubleday and Co., Inc., 1978.

Council Effectiveness Evaluated

by Marliss Rogers

"Is the Lord among us or not?" (Ex 7:17)

Like other organizations, parish pastoral councils need occasional check-ups to maintain effectiveness. It is healthy for council members to engage in periodic reflection on how well they are using the gifts of the Spirit to bring the parish into deeper community and a more dynamic ministry and mission. Parish leaders are not called to perpetuate their own viewpoints or personal desires, nor to engage in a struggle for power, but to enable and to serve.

Evaluating parish leadership in an honest and loving way is not disloyal; rather, it helps the council become more effective and faithful servants and stewards of parish resources. Rev. J. Gordon Myers describes the purpose of evaluation in this inspiring way: "Evaluation is the ongoing discernment of a group's vocation; its ministerial call to holiness. It is first and foremost a spiritual exercise, enabling the group to tell the whole truth about itself in the presence of a loving God."[1]

Evaluation is also a necessary first step in planning. Assessing the effectiveness of the council as leadership ministry is an important part of evaluating all parish ministries. It is good to remember that evaluation is always going on. Most of us are familiar with the council meeting that continues in the parking lot when important issues are not resolved. An evaluation process can provide an orderly and caring method for honest assessment, and give integrity to the church's desire to be faithful to its call and mission.

In *Evaluating Ministry,* Jill Hudson suggests a theological basis for evaluation:

> Faith and covenant are the foundation for ministry evaluation. Faith that trusts in the Holy Spirit to guide and direct our deliberations, faith in the inherent goodness of each as well as the potential for failure, faith that God's forgiveness is extended to us all when we fall short of God's intent for our ministry. Covenant in that we are bound to one another through Christ and called to partnership in mission. All love requires accountability. God loves us but calls us into account for the covenant we have made with God.[2]

What should be evaluated and how? Both content and process of council meetings should be considered. Accountability to the parish and its mission as well as collaboration with pastor and staff also ought to be evaluated. The spiritual development of the council is another important matter for review, so that the council will grow in faith and wisdom.

Both formal and informal evaluation are needed. Brief, informal evaluation can take place after each council meeting. Suggested questions are:

- *Did the meeting accomplish its goals? Was there movement on the agenda?*
- *Were council members truly listening to one another? Responding?*
- *How were decisions made? Did council members feel good about them?*
- *Were prayer and reflection integral to the meeting?*
- *What is the Holy Spirit calling us to be and do as a result of our meeting?*

It is important that a more formal evaluation of the council's activities take place at the last meeting of the year. This evaluation session begins with prayer and individual reflection, then honest dialogue, with the goal being mutual perception about the strengths and weaknesses of the parish pastoral council. Some suggestions for dialogue are:

- *What decision making process do we use? How well does it work?*
- *Do we receive enough information to make wise decisions?*
- *As a result of council decisions, have we become more centered on the mission of Jesus and gospel values?*
- *Are we living up to our mission statement? Where are we with our pastoral plan?*
- *As a council, did we manifest real accountability to the parish or did we tend to be a "leadership elite"? Are we truly servant leaders?*
- *What method do we use to select council members? Does this method result in capable leadership? New leadership?*
- *What contributions have we made to diocesan goals during the past year?*
- *Do we actively participate in the formation and approval of the annual budget?*
- *How did we as parish leaders help the parish to make an impact on the community? Did we set an example for welcoming, evangelizing behavior?*
- *How well do we work together and support one another?*
- *What should we have done differently?*

It is best when council evaluation happens as part of a regular process in which the council (and other parish groups) engage. The parish should also be given an opportunity to provide feedback to the parish pastoral council about its ministry and goals. Too often, councilors fail to see accountability to the parish as part of their responsibility.

Is There Life after Evaluation?

Only if there has been clarity about what will happen as a result of the evaluation process. Evaluation is useless unless conclusions are taken seriously and they are incorporated into the future operation of the council.

> A thorough self-evaluation will reveal both strengths and deficiencies in various aspects of the council's life. A maturing council will, of course, accept the challenge and deal with the deficiencies as part of its own continuing program of renewal. . . . Self-evaluation and fraternal correction have been part of the Catholic tradition for centuries."[3]

Council members must be prepared for change as a result of assessing its ministry. New realizations will emerge from the process, which can lead to adjustments in how the council functions. New directions may open up and new forms put into place.

Councilors will also see their relationships to one another in a new light. Commitment to the gospel and the church's mission will be revitalized as reflective dialogue continues. And evaluation helps parish pastoral council members to see that their efforts do make a difference in parish life.

This wonderful quotation from the United Methodist Church offers a spiritual outlook about evaluation:

> Evaluation is natural to the human experience. Evaluation is one of God's ways of bringing the history of the past into dialogue with the hope for the future. . . . Surrounded by God's grace and the crowd of witnesses in the faith, we can look at our past unafraid and from its insights eagerly face the future with new possibilities."[4]

Truthful, prayerful assessment can lead to renewed direction for the council and spiritual growth for individual council members. It is wise to keep in mind, however, that the truth can hurt. People are "earthen vessels" who require care and kindness when evaluative interaction takes place.

If used properly and within the context of the development in faith of the whole parish, evaluation will serve to help build up the body of Christ, not contribute to its division, so that all will recognize that God is truly among us, always. The following two forms can be used effectively in this manner.

Notes

[1] J. Gordon Myers, quoted in *The Gathering.* (out of print.)

[2] Hudson, Jill, *Evaluating Ministry,* Alban Institute, 1992.

[3] Rademacher, Rev. William and Marliss Rogers, *New Practical Guide for Parish Councils,* Twenty Third Publications, 1988.

[4] *Theological and Theoretical Foundations for Evaluating Ministry,* Division of Ordained Ministry, United Methoidst Church.

ASSESSMENT OF COUNCIL MEETINGS

Thinking of the way in which your council functions, score each of the following items by placing the appropriate letter in the blank in front of the item, using the following scale: Y = Yes; S = Sometimes; N = Never

1. _____ Most of the agenda is set at the end of the previous meeting.
2. _____ It's easy to get new items on the agenda.
3. _____ There is good coordination between meetings and reminders of reports due.
4. _____ Personal conflicts are smoothed over or avoided.
5. _____ If decisions are made, it is clear who is to carry them out.
6. _____ At each meeting, we review the business of the previous meeting.
7. _____ The same problems keep coming up meeting after meeting.
8. _____ We know what kinds of decisions we should make.
9. _____ We consider many alternative solutions prior to making a decision to take action.
10. _____ Motions suggesting action are made only after discussion.
11. _____ People talk differently outside the meeting than they do during the meeting.
12. _____ Council members check with each other to make sure they understand what is said.
13. _____ Each individual speaks for him/herself rather than generalizing with statements like "we think" or "our people believe," or "everybody says."
14. _____ Our council understands its purpose.
15. _____ Checking the agenda items to be considered in the next meeting, and the ordering of these items is the last item of business.
16. _____ At our meetings, chairs are so arranged that we can all see each other's faces.
17. _____ During our meetings we support each other's ministry.

18. _____ We hold ourselves accountable to the parish.
19. _____ Prayer and growth in spiritual values are goals each meeting.
20. _____ There is a sense of community in our council.

PARISH COUNCIL COMMITTEE EVALUATION

Circle the number closest to your perception for each statement, with 5 signifying the highest level of agreement

SPIRITUAL

1. Membership on this committee has been a rewarding spiritual experience.

1   2   3   4   5

2. The committee prays together regularly.

1   2   3   4   5

3. We have rap sessions at least once a year to share what membership on this committee has meant in our personal, family and parish lives.

1   2   3   4   5

4. This committee recognizes its responsibility to assist the pastor and council in determining what spiritual needs are apparent in the parish.

1   2   3   4   5

5. Our committee participates in days of recollection, retreats, workshops, etc.

1   2   3   4   5

6. We look for ways in which our committee activities can challenge us to grow in Christ, and we bond with one another in friendship.

1   2   3   4   5

MEMBERSHIP and TASKS

1. We prepare helpful materials for the council to keep abreast of our activities, including at least two alternatives for any proposal to the council.

1   2   3   4   5

2. Any actionable items brought into committee are promptly assigned and worked to a solution.

1   2   3   4   5

3. The members of this committee cooperate well with one another.

1   2   3   4   5

4. We rotate committee membership whenever possible and provide leadership training.

1   2   3   4   5

5. We make an effort to get more people involved in our committee and seek to identify and develop their gifts.

1   2   3   4   5

6. We discern our committee leadership in a prayerful process.

1   2   3   4   5

RELATIONSHIPS

1. Our relationship with the parish council is one of interdependence.

1   2   3   4   5

2. We envision our committee relationship with the parish as being an enabling one, and we seek regular feedback from parishioners on our programs and projects.

1   2   3   4   5

3. We attempt to reach out to make people feel welcome and comfortable at our committee activities.

1   2   3   4   5

4. We try to include an ecumenical dimension in our committee activities.

1   2   3   4   5

INVOLVEMENT IN PASTORAL PLANNING

1. We keep abreast of what other council committees are doing and how it relates to our committee ministry.

1   2   3   4   5

2. Our committee's goals are based on the parish mission statement and the parish council goals.

1   2   3   4   5

3. Our goals each have objectives, with timed programs to reach the objectives.

1   2   3   4   5

4. We regularly evaluate our programs and projects.

1   2   3   4   5

5. Our committee meetings are well planned.

$$1 \qquad 2 \qquad 3 \qquad 4 \qquad 5$$

6. We engage in long-term planning, in cooperation with other committees and the council.

$$1 \qquad 2 \qquad 3 \qquad 4 \qquad 5$$

RENEWAL AND UPDATE

1. A high priority on our agenda is continued renewal and update of our methods and vision.

$$1 \qquad 2 \qquad 3 \qquad 4 \qquad 5$$

2. Vatican II and bishops' pastorals are one source of education for the members of our committee.

$$1 \qquad 2 \qquad 3 \qquad 4 \qquad 5$$

3. We appreciate that committee results are often slow and hard to measure. We see and point out changes in parish life which have resulted from our work, and help people deal with change.

$$1 \qquad 2 \qquad 3 \qquad 4 \qquad 5$$

4. We read and discuss material from the (arch) diocesan offices. We also communicate our insights about our specific ministry to the diocesan offices and contribute to their goals.

$$1 \qquad 2 \qquad 3 \qquad 4 \qquad 5$$